TRUE STORIES OF
RESCUE AND SURVIVAL

TRUE STORIES OF RESCUE AND SURVIVAL

CANADA'S UNKNOWN HEROES

CAROLYN MATTHEWS

DUNDURN PRESS
TORONTO

Editor: Michael Carroll
Copy-editor: Allison Hirst
Design: Courtney Horner
Printer: Marquis

Library and Archives Canada Cataloguing in Publication

Matthews, Carolyn
    True stories of rescue and survival : Canada's unknown
heroes / by Carolyn Matthews.

 Includes bibliographical references.
ISBN 978-1-55002-851-5

    1. Heroes--Canada--Biography--Juvenile literature.
2. Canada--Biography--Juvenile literature. I. Title.

FC25.M493 2008   j971.009'9   C2008-905921-2

1   2   3   4   5   12   11   10   09   08

 Conseil des Arts du Canada / Canada Council for the Arts

 Canadä

ONTARIO ARTS COUNCIL
CONSEIL DES ARTS DE L'ONTARIO

We acknowledge the support of the **Canada Council for the Arts** and the **Ontario Arts Council** for our publishing program. We also acknowledge the financial support of the **Government of Canada** through the **Book Publishing Industry Development Program** and **The Association for the Export of Canadian Books**, and the **Government of Ontario** through the **Ontario Book Publishers Tax Credit program**, and the **Ontario Media Development Corporation**.

Care has been taken to trace the ownership of copyright material used in this book. The author and the publisher welcome any information enabling them to rectify any references or credits in subsequent editions.

J. Kirk Howard, President

Printed and bound in Canada.
Printed on recycled paper.

www.dundurn.com

Dundurn Press
3 Church Street, Suite 500
Toronto, Ontario, Canada
M5E 1M2

Gazelle Book Services Limited
White Cross Mills
High Town, Lancaster, England
LA1 4XS

Dundurn Press
2250 Military Road
Tonawanda, NY
U.S.A. 14150

For Dave Griffiths

Contents

Acknowledgements

To the heroes inside the covers of this book — and to all of you who are not because space did not permit — thanks so much for your time and patience in helping me tell these stories.

Thanks to members of the Parliament Street Writers — Sarah, Laurie, Vern, Simon, Susan, and Ruth — for your editing, and your good company!

Introduction

When a young man's small plane splits in half after smashing into a mountain in the Rockies, his fleeting thought is: *My mother's going to be pissed at me. She's always saying things like, Jeez, Kurt, should you be jumping off that cliff?*

Near Newfoundland's treacherous coast, a drowning fisherman watches a rescue technician being hoisted down to save him, but he disappears under the water. "The rescue guys, they killed one of their own" are his words. Afterwards, when the same "rescue guy" climbs down the cliffs to him, he whispers, "I seen a ghost."

Search and Rescue Technicians with the Armed Forces use words like *honour* and *pride*. One young man stated how proud, how patriotic he felt when he wore his uniform, Canadian flag on his left shoulder — his pleasure in serving his country and fellow man.

"There is honour in being in the Army," young Norm Penny stated. "This work gives me the opportunity to believe in, and to stand for something. It's a good feeling. I'm proud to be a soldier. We'll do anything to rescue people: mountain climbing, medical help, boating, parachuting, scuba diving, helicopter hoisting … we do our absolute best to save lives."

The rescuees I interviewed also heaped praise on the Military and spoke admiringly of the men and women who work for it. Police officers too; their often painstaking work is out of the spotlight and not generally appreciated by the public — not in the way that busting a drug ring or arresting a suspect at a crime scene might be. But officers never give up — *Crime will not go unpunished* said one.

Civilians, too, train themselves and make huge sacrifices to help others.

Canada's heroes and their stories range widely: a Navy diver and explosives expert defuses bombs in the Afghan desert. Other rescue stories take place across Canada's vast and inhospitable landscape: a jump into an Arctic blizzard; a helicopter long-line rescue on British Columbian mountains; a child lost in the forests of New Brunswick; fishermen perishing in the cruel North Atlantic; a married couple missing from the streets of Vancouver; and not least, a prize goat rescued from Ontario's Welland Canal.

If it is human nature to want heroes, then perhaps it is possible to influence who we choose. These stories are an attempt to do just this.

Courtesy of the Canadian Amphibian Search Team, Winnipeg.

Search and Rescue volunteers train under the direction of the RCMP in Brandon, Manitoba.

1 Buried in an Arctic Blizzard

Nunavut, April 2005

"I think maybe you should check out the weather," suggests one of his mates, and the commercial helicopter pilot glances up at a clear blue sky.

"Looks pretty good to me right now," he replies, but knows he'll carefully check out the long-range forecast before he takes off for Kelowna, British Columbia.

Jason Brown has just finished air-lifting drills at a mining site in Ferguson, Nunavut. He's 300 miles south of the Arctic Circle, and the flight to Kelowna will take him 19 hours flying time, or three whole days.

Clear skies are expected for the next eight to ten hours, then bad stuff will hit — this forecast gives him pause, but Jason is not too concerned since he's familiar with this remote area of Canada and its weather. After all, this is where he works most of the time. He says goodbye to his mates and takes off. An hour and half later he stops to fuel up with gasoline he's carried on board — it will get rid of some of his weight. He lifts off again, still under clear, sunny skies.

Half an hour later he hits fierce winds. Gusts whip up walls of snow 1,000 feet in the air. One minute he's over a lake, and the next, he can't even see it. The whole world has gone white. Prickles of apprehension run down his spine as he ponders what to do. Go up above the bad weather? — If he does, he'll have to climb up to 3,000 feet, and that's too high. Something else: He can't use instruments for flying, he actually has to see.

Yes! There's an opening in the thick layer of cloud. Okay, he'll go down into it, land, and wait for the storm to pass — maybe no more than a couple of hours. Then he can lift off and fly away.

He approaches the hole in the cloud, but as he does, it starts to disappear. Now he's in the situation he wanted to avoid — caught right in the middle of a total white-out where he can't see a thing! He doesn't know where anything is; can't tell which way is up and which is down. There's not even a tree to help him because he's still 50 miles north of the tree line — no visual reference at all. Next thing he knows, he's flying into the ground.

The snow gets thicker and thicker and the opening in the cloud disappears entirely. Where's the ground? Where's the ground? Suddenly he's hit it. He's crashed hard onto an icy lake. The helicopter skids hit ice. The little aircraft bounces up four or five hundred metres in the air before it bumps down again on the skids. This time Jason manages a controlled landing.

He's stunned for a moment, palms sweaty and heart racing. Gusting winds hurl snow about the copter, and his dismal thought is that it won't be long before he's buried in it. With a hollow feeling in the pit of his stomach he knows he won't be taking off again any time soon.

Still strapped in his pilot's seat, he doesn't freak out. After all, he's a seasoned training pilot and used to all kinds of difficult situations. He'll

FASCINATING FACT
Measuring in Knots

The Navy has always measured speed in knots, a practice followed by pilots, and used from very early times. Aviation traditionally has followed what the marine world practises, since, like shipping, it is an international activity. And because land transport rules are different from one nation to another, it seemed a sensible idea to use nautical rules and terms as much as possible. This way everyone knew what was going on.

Knots, port, starboard, 4-ring captains, cabin pursers, red/green navigation lights — all came from the sea. A knot is one nautical mile per hour, and a nautical mile is almost identical to a minute of latitude. This helps with navigation. A nautical mile is the same if travelling by air or on the water. All maritime and aeronautical maps are measured in nautical miles. But pilots and meteorologists in some countries — like Russia — use MPS (metres per second) instead for wind speeds. In fact, Russians use only metres and kilometres. Other countries measure wind speed in miles per hour (MPH).

just have to wait — and hope he won't freeze!

He checks that there's no damage to his helicopter — or to himself — then sits back and waits. And waits. Snow blows thickly all about him. Winds tear about the helicopter and shriek across the empty landscape.

As time passes he starts to worry. He has been in the Arctic before, but never in a wind this fierce. He figures it must be hurtling at about 40 knots.

Does he hunker down, or leap back into the air? — So hard to know what to do. He decides to stay put and wait out the weather, but he must go outside to the chopper's cargo area to get his sleeping gear. He finds it, puts it on the ground, and wedges it with his leg so it won't blow away. Then he looks for more of his stuff — one thing he'll need for sure is a spare battery. As he reaches for it, a violent gust grabs his sleeping bag right out of his hand and blows it away. Jason stares after it in dismay as it disappears into the snow. Now there is no way he can keep warm. His thoughts are bleak as he stares out at the white landscape. He puts out a hand, but can't even see it in front of his face. No way he can go and look for the sleeping bag — of course not! He's heard stories of others who have gone out in conditions like this and never made it back; next morning they are found standing up frozen in the snow. Guys who do go out in these conditions tie themselves with rope to a corner of a building or their aircraft so they can be sure to get back.

Back in the helicopter, he tries to stay warm but there's nothing to help him. He takes stock of what he has: enough fuel to keep the chopper running at ten-minute intervals for about 24 hours. After that, he'll be out of heat completely. These thoughts remind him that he's totally alone.

His first radio communication tells him that a five-day blizzard is forecast and he's landed right in the middle of it. Jason thinks about spending five days in minus 25 degrees or lower temperatures, in a helicopter with no heat, and with no way to warm himself. He has nothing to eat. It will be the end of him. His thoughts remain bleak as he turns again to his radio. He calls the mining company. He asks them to declare an emergency because he knows that all by himself he'll never get out of here alive.

The Starfield Exploration Mining Company in Nunavut calls the Rescue Coordination Centre in Trenton, Ontario: *A chopper has gone down in the Arctic.*

Master Corporal Brian Decaire is a young Search and Rescue Technician (SAR Tech) with the Armed Forces, stationed at 435 Squadron in Winnipeg. He's on call, but socializing with his friends in a downtown hotel in Winnipeg. The evening is interrupted by his pager, its message telling him that he's about to be launched on a search and rescue mission. Immediately he calls up the operations centre to acknowledge that he received the page, and to find out what it's about. He turns to his friends.

"A helicopter pilot's gone down over Boland Lake near Rankin Inlet," he says. "The pilot is okay, but he's stuck in a blizzard. We'll fly out and drop him enough supplies to last him until the weather clears. Be back tomorrow morning — latest by afternoon. I'll call you when I'm home again." He takes off to join his rescue team and begin preparations for the mission. He's a rookie with only one search and rescue mission under his belt and it's exciting to have been given this one. The mission sounds straightforward: A flight of about two and a half hours in a Hercules C-130 from Winnipeg to the spot where the pilot is stranded, 200 miles west of Rankin Inlet. Once there, they'll drop the guy some supplies and come home.

The Rescue Centre orders a Hercules rescue plane to fly out from Winnipeg to the spot where Jason has gone down. The time is half past six in the evening and the distance to travel is 700 nautical miles. Captain Kashe Bryngleson is the aircraft commander, and Sergeant Darcy St.

FASCINATING FACT
Survival Toboggans and What They Contain — A SAR Tech's Account

As Canadian Forces Search and Rescue crews, we carry different types of survival kits that can be air-dropped to survivors on the ground:
• A food and water kit that contains: A box of ten individually packed meals (IMPs similar to American MRE meals — ready to eat). A small camp stove, some camp fuel for it, a pot for cooking, and a few other accessories.
• A clothing kit containing a parka, mitts, warm boots, wind pants, a warm sweater, long underwear, an Arctic sleeping bag, and a large tarp for building an improvised shelter.
• A survival toboggan that contains: A large tent, and all of the supplies listed in the above two kits. (All of the equipment is stored in a military metal toboggan.)
• Sometimes we improvise and fill barrels with survival items. This happens only when, or if, pre-packaged kits don't meet the requirements of the situation.

Laurent is the Search and Rescue team leader for the mission.

"We're given more details as we get our gear ready," Brian says. "We have to rig the supplies so they can be dropped from the aircraft with a supply parachute. What I'm hearing makes me start to worry about the guy and I want to get out there to him — fast. He's already been on the ground for 12 hours and the power in his chopper must be going down. No heat so he'll quickly become hypothermic. He'll be running out of food, and his water will quickly freeze. He'll become dehydrated and not be able to help himself. There's something else — I'm worried about his state of mind. We're taught that the worst enemy of survival is loneliness. Twelve hours in his situation can be mentally draining — and he could be there much longer. Put all these things together and it's a bad situation.

"As the sun begins its descent over the horizon, the Hercules arrives over the frozen lake. Darcy asks the captain to turn on his lights so Jason can better see us. 'We'll light up the sky with flares for him,' I said. 'We'll drop him a radio and some supplies.'

"The two of us prepare all the gear in a survival toboggan. Our goal is to have it land as close to the helicopter as possible, but not actually hit it — something that's not easy when the wind is blowing at 50 or 60 knots. First thing we do is drop him the radio so he can save the helicopter's battery power.

"We drop it — great! — It lands quite close to him. 'Bull's Eye!' I yell. 'Can you go and get it?' But Jason says he can't see it for all the blowing snow and sounds pretty unnerved at the thought of going out into the blizzard to get it. He

> **FASCINATING FACT**
> **Water Supplies in the Arctic**
>
> The difficulty of maintaining water supplies in Arctic conditions is that liquid will freeze, and a stranded person without water will suck on ice. If he does, it will hasten the onset of hypothermia because he is using his body heat to melt the ice. Most people don't realize they are getting dehydrated as they normally would in warmer climates.

> **FASCINATING FACT**
> **Parachute Flares**
>
> Flares use white phosphorous and magnesium for fuel. Both these ingredients burn very hot and bright under a parachute, and light up the sky as they fall. Each one has a two-million-candle power that lasts for five minutes.

probably can't see the chopper when he's more than just a few feet from it. We hear him mutter that he knows it's out there somewhere; that he has to go out and get it, but what if he doesn't get back? He's got a baby at home … is he going to get out of this alive?

"*Hey, don't worry*, we radio back. *We'll get you out of here man. We'll guide you while you're out there and be right behind you. We'll light up the sky for you!* We talk him into going out to try and get the things we've dropped for him. He goes out, manages to find the toboggan, and hauls it back to his chopper.

"Next, we drop him a survival toboggan with a Coleman stove, lantern, a tent, sleeping bags, and food and water in it. It weighs 300 pounds, and almost hits Jason's helicopter. But the poor guy seems a bit bummed out.

"'Can you get the tent set up?' Darcy asks him. 'Can you get the lantern and stove going? What camping supplies do you have? And what kind of sleeping bag? How much food?'"

"'Thanks,' Jason radios back. 'But I … don't know if I can set it all up … I'm not trained in this survival stuff and it's getting rough here …' There's a long pause, then he asks 'Can you come down to me?'"

"'Oh!' Darcy looks at me. 'You know, I've got a feeling he's not going to manage it,' he says. 'Even we SAR Techs would have a hard time in the conditions he's in. Oh man!'"

FASCINATING FACT
Risk Assessment for a Jump — Questions SAR Techs Ask Themselves

How hard is the surface, and how strong the winds? What is the horizontal visibility? Will the weather get worse, and for how long? The crew in the Hercules knows the winds are at 48 knots. This is two and a half times above normal training limits for parachuting at night. They know that visibility is severely diminished.

They know they have no recognizable features on the ground — only Jason's aircraft. They also know they might have trouble reaching their intended landing zone in the winds.

The two SAR Techs fall silent, each busy with their own thoughts. This is a really big decision to make. Each man knows that, on the one hand, Jason is alive and not injured. He has some food and water, and he has shelter. But — what might happen if they don't get to him? Will he be able to get the stove going? Will he get lost in the blizzard when he goes out to pick up more supplies? He might become hypothermic. He might be such a rough state that he can't help himself … he could even die.

Jason repeats that he can't see anything and that he doesn't have good survival skills. He knows the crew can see his beacon lights, but he can't see them, and he won't be able to unless they are right on top of him. He feels trapped and isolated in the scary white world.

"Look," Darcy says, "we won't let you down. We'll shut off communication for a minute and then get back to you. Hold tight."

Okay, now for Plan B: The crew makes a risk assessment for a jump — a desperate last resort to help the stranded man.

Five minutes pass before the SAR Techs come back on air to him — the longest silence of Jason's life. "Okay, Jason," comes Darcy's voice. "We're coming down to sit out the storm with you."

Tears well up in Jason's eyes at the news, but his relief is immediately mixed with fear for these strangers: They can't possibly know how bad the conditions are on the ground — so much worse than what they can see from up there.

Above in the Hercules, the two SAR Techs begin making preparations to parachute down.

"I start thinking about the conditions for this jump," Darcy says. "And about our training; Brian is brand-new in the SAR world, and this will only be his second operational jump. We don't parachute in winds above 25 knots during training because it's just not worth the risk. It's up to the SAR team leader to decide if the winds are too high for the mission. Right now they're double our training limits. It's night-time. There's blowing snow and no visibility. If we jump, we'll be seriously risking our lives. We continue to discuss the severity of the conditions; about the possibility of getting injured on the jump — like breaking a femur — and of course, this means the possibility of being killed."

"Holy cow, this is crazy." Brian looks at the senior SAR Tech. "If we get injured, there's no one to get *us* out. That'll be it — we'll be on our own. We'll be done for. But if we don't go down and get to this guy, and he dies, it's going to be on our conscience."

Darcy listens. He thinks about wind direction. He knows their aircraft is facing into it, so they can jump the same way. But on the ground — well, he just doesn't know. He's reasonably experienced, but Brian is not.

FASCINATING FACT
Jumping into the Wind

The difficult part about jumping in the type of wind that exists for the two SAR Techs is to determine how far upwind they should exit the aircraft.

The jump master decides the timing for the drop. If a parachutist jumps too early he can be blown right past his target. Too late, and he won't make it to the target.

When exiting the plane, the wind should be at his back. When he lands, he wants to turn into it, to slow his forward progression. When these SAR Techs turn into wind, they are blown backwards at a high speed.

Brian's thoughts are racing. He thinks how, during training, he jumps to suitable drop zones. The weather is okay — nothing like this — and if he does get hurt, the Hercules aircraft can land and take him to an airport where there is a hospital nearby — he has ground support already in place. Here, the only support the two of them have is each other. Jason wants them to go down to him, but he's telling them about a thick blizzard on the ground. His thoughts go round and round. He starts thinking that he can't do this easily; that it's actually extremely difficult. It's right out of his usual commuting limits.

"Just the thought of it makes me nervous," he says. "In these kinds of situations, no one can order someone else to jump. It has to be agreed to by both SAR Techs. Darcy asks me a couple of times when we're getting ready, am I okay with doing this? If I say no, we won't go. I think the big part of our decision is that if we don't go, and this guy dies, it will be on our conscience. Our mission is to help people and save them. It's our job, and it's what we get paid to do … I remember when I was in the Infantry. You kind of sit back and dream about all these cool rescues you're going on. You're young. You're going to write all these awesome books about your adventures … But, this is our job, we're here to help.

"Darcy and I stare at each other. Then I say, 'You're the boss. It's your call. If you think we can do it, I'm on for it.' Am I nervous? *Oh yeah!* On board our aircraft are two pilots, a flight engineer, a navigator, and a load master who's in charge of all the gear. He makes sure everything is secured in the back of the Hercules. But we also have to look after our own gear — it's a coordinated team. There's a flurry of activity as we all prepare.

"We're almost ready. We throw on all our winter gear — parkas and wind pants and fleeces. Then we put on our parachutes — they are the kind made to carry a lot of weight. It's a hefty load. I weigh 200 pounds and I'm carrying at least 100 pounds of gear that includes medical supplies, snowshoes, all kinds of survival stuff — and extra water, which is very heavy.

"The sun has set. We're dressed and ready to go. I'm nervous. Winds are gusting at 45 knots. Darcy drops the drift indicator light to assess the strength and direction of the wind. It disappears in the blizzard. We're jumping from 2,500 feet. It's dark so we need flares to jump with, or we won't see a thing. We keep dropping more of them to help us see the canopy, and to see the ground when we land.

"The two flares go first. We're to wait ten seconds, then follow. I'm on the ramp … I'm scared, but I've got to suck it up. The sensible part of me is asking, *Are you sure you want to do this?* My nerves are really going and I'm thinking: *Holy cow, I hope I get out of this one! I hope I get on the ground in one piece and everything's okay.* The scariest part is the jump — really scary. Usually it's not, because you're dropping into jump zones on airfields, and you've got escape plans. No escape with this one. And, oh man, it is cold!

"I know Darcy is very worried about me. He's been doing this for ten years, but me … better stop thinking …

"I'm ready. I jump. The wind is at my back and I'm dropping fast … I've never gone that fast. Hey, it's a ride, and I'm motoring — just like a Ferrari. Darcy's right behind me. I just want to get to the helicopter and land close to it. As I get nearer, the wind changes direction. I'm flying into blowing snow — huge layers of it. I can't tell the horizon from the ground. Everywhere I look is white, white, and more white. How far down is it? With the kind of wind that's blowing and the weight we're jumping with, it's like, *oh man, where's the ground?* Now I'm getting blown away from the helicopter. I do my best to turn into the wind to slow down my forward progression but I'm being blown backwards. I keep struggling, and it slows me down a bit. I put my knees and feet together and try to relax; to let ground come to me.

"Suddenly I hit — hard! But I can't control my chute and I'm being dragged. I'm blown about 200 metres before I can cut it away. Finally I'm clear of it, and I get up. I peer through the whiteness that's swamping me and can just make out the helicopter. It seems very far. I need to get to it. I *have* to get to it. I mean, I can't get lost in this blizzard! Normally when we land, we call up as soon as possible to tell the crew we've landed safely. But I decide to get to the helicopter first because I don't want to get lost in the blowing snow. Once I get there I will call up. All this time I've been flying under canopy, and haven't had radio contact with anyone."

On the ground Jason anxiously watches. There is little he can see. But something's out there — must be the first guy. He's coming out of the sky in the middle of the night! Jason can just make out a figure flying over his helicopter and landing a hundred feet from it. What great aim!

Three to four seconds after Brian has gone down, Darcy jumps.

"I'm coming down … down," the senior SAR Tech says. "It's horrible. It's difficult and it's painful. I'm trying to follow Brian in, but I lose him. I've lost visual reference. I feel all disoriented and don't know where I am, don't know where the chopper is, where Brian is … I think he must have lost his strobe light …

"I thought I saw him turn early, so I'm thinking, *okay, he must be about here*. I look about me and can see the lights on the helicopter. It's wrapped in a low-level blizzard about two to three hundred feet thick. It's really wild with wind blowing snow all over the place. Above us the sky is clear.

"I did a turn early, thinking that's where Brian is, and I can land with him. Then I completely lose him. I'm falling. I can't see the helicopter, can't see the wind direction … *What to do now?* I can't turn. If I do I'll go in a bank and roll. If I roll, then land like that, I could easily break both my femurs.

"I'm entering a low-level blizzard and all I can see are walls of white and have to work hard to keep a cool mind. My altimeter is reading zero. It seems to be staying like this for a long time so only one thing can be happening: my forward speed must be incredibly fast and decreasing my descent. But I should hit the ground any moment. *Where is it? When am I going to hit?* I can't see a thing. I'm scared. I see my strobe lights blink on and off and when they blink on I get sort of blinded. I feel the wind

---

FASCINATING FACT
The Seriousness of a Fractured Femur

The femur is one of the largest and strongest bones in the body. It is the thigh bone, extending from the hip right down to the knee joint. It is a very strong bone and it takes tremendous force to cause it to fracture. When it does, it is a very traumatic injury, the typical kind a parachutist might get if he doesn't land properly. There is an immediate large loss of blood and death can occur quite rapidly.

at my back and know I have to turn into it, but it's not the time to be turning … I'll be vertical to the ground and my parachute will drive me straight into it …

"I still can't tell where the ground is, even though my altimeter keeps reading zero … then suddenly the ground jumps up and hits me in the feet! The wind is knocked right out of my lungs and my brain feels rattled. I roll, feet and knees together. I'm being dragged by my parachute that's acting like a giant sail. I can't collapse it; I'm all tangled up in the lines and can't cut the things. They're everywhere: caught on my equipment, around my legs, my neck … usual procedure is to cut away the handle and jettison the parachute. If I do that, I just know I'll be left hanging by my neck. I'll choke. The wind, the snow, the hard icy surface of the lake — all of it hits and I'm bumping around. It's an intense moment for me.

"I'm still being dragged … I'm tired … so tired … I have to collapse my chute. If I pull in some critical lines it will collapse, but it's not working. *Not working!* I've got to stop this crazy ride. Okay, desperate times call for desperate measure — I'll have to use my safety knife to cut away my chute. I don't want to do it — I've become attached to my parachute: it's carried me safely down to the ground so many times. But I must. I take my knife and start chopping lines indiscriminately. I try the left riser — that's nylon webbing attached to all lines — but no luck. I try the right side, and the razor cuts through the riser like butter. My chute collapses instantly and everything stops, except for the howling wind. I take a deep breath of freezing air. I can't believe I'm still alive — maybe I'm dreaming?

"I start hauling in my gear. I think I can relax for a moment. But no, I have to put things away and take care of my gear … I have to radio the Herc to tell them where I am, and that I'm okay.

"But where am I? Where's the chopper? How far is it? Where's Brian? — Where is he? *How* is he? I radio the plane to give them information about myself, and to ask about him. 'We don't know,' the aircraft commander says, anxiety in his voice. 'We haven't heard from him.'

"Oh! More than 15 minutes must have passed since both of us jumped. It's a long time for the crew in the Hercules to wait for communication from a SAR Tech — they usually hear in five to ten minutes. They'll be worried about what's going on down here. I'm worried too — worried about my mate. I'm the team leader. I made the decision…. What if …? The very worst part for me right now is not my own horrible situation, but that Brian hasn't come on the radio.

"I start walking straight into the wind. With me I'm carrying my collapsed parachute and all my survival gear — about 110 pounds. Have to get to the chopper … I have a general idea where it is, and know that it's far. I keep walking, and it's so very cold! I can't control my mind and start thinking about this walk to get to the chopper; about staying in the Arctic, the anguish of not knowing what happened to my partner, and the big decision I made to do this jump. That gets me thinking about Jason and what if we hadn't jumped to him. He's a fellow with very little experience and what could he have done to survive without us? Even if he'd been able to go out from his chopper on his own and get some of the supplies we'd dropped for him — I mean, it's a big storm — what would have happened to him? Even if he'd gone just 15 metres from his chopper, he could easily have got lost. I know all the stories about what happens to people when they can't find their way back. Then — could he have set up camp for himself? Light the stove, the lantern, put up the tent … and what about us? I'd made the decision to jump … my thoughts are racing on like this.

"Someone's come on the radio. Hey, it's Brian — am I relieved!

"'Shoot a flare,' I tell him. Brian can't possibly know how badly I need help: I'm barely standing upright in the middle of nowhere. The wind's blowing the snow right in my face so it's not very practical for me to try and get out my GPS and punch in a bunch of numbers in the wind. Besides, electronic devices — they don't always work. I just keep walking; just want to get there.

"I wait for the flares. Usually they shoot up two or three hundred feet in the air, but these barely rise above the horizon. I stare at them, dismayed: They show just how far I am from the helicopter. If I'd been injured and couldn't walk; if I couldn't contact anyone, what would happen to me?

"It takes me 90 minutes to two hours to get to the chopper — hard to tell how much time passes. I walk and walk, straight into the wind. I'm bent over with the 100 pounds I'm carrying, and am tempted to leave my parachute behind. Better not: I might need it for a shelter or for a blanket, but hope I don't have to.

"'Darcy!' Brian's voice comes as a shout. When I emerge out of the whiteness, he exclaims

'Hey, you look like some apparition!' And he smiles his relief. 'You're like the abominable snowman suddenly appearing out of the white.'"

"Yeah, well …"

'Your face is completely iced up. And your eyebrows, your lips, your nose …'

"I tell him never mind about that. All I know is that I'm bent over with the weight of more than 100 pounds of gear on my back and can't go a step further. And we have to try to set up a tent right away.

"It takes us about three hours to do this because of the wind and everything flying everywhere. We get the stove and lanterns going. We roll out our sleeping bags and try to sleep. It's impossible. I'm feeling traumatized. It's like, *uhhh!* But at the same time, I thank my lucky stars I'm alive. The conditions are very harsh. We have to sleep and live in a tent and we don't know for how long. We have to keep working all the time to improve the camp so we can live in it. There's Jason: he seems worried. I think he's feeling guilty he asked us to come. We tell him this is our job; he's not even to think about it. I mean, we have the gear. We have skills, the training … but it's very challenging."

"By 4:30 in the morning we pass out," Jason says. "By seven, we know it's not going to work."

"We wake up — that's if we slept at all," says Brian. "And the day is even worse. Winds gust at 60 knots and blow snow so thick we can't see a thing outside — we're blind. We use a satellite phone to contact the JRCC to ask about a weather forecast. It's depressing: they can't tell us when the blizzard will subside. We struggle up and into the freezing cold. Winds shriek. As though in rage, heavy snow hits at us — hard. We have a three-man tent set up, but it's too small, so we get to work to put up a bigger one — a tent we can use for cooking and drying out our clothes. But more problems: We can't get the bigger tent to stay up properly because of all the snow and the wind hitting it. We get out our knives and saws and build up snow walls to protect it — sort of like building an igloo — but the snow is not the right kind for that, so we put together a snow box: We cut blocks of ice out of the windswept lake. We use them to build up walls around that area where we're cutting them from. Once they are high enough, we try to put up the tent inside them.

"It's very, very cold. Our tent gets blown all over the place and the poles are breaking. We have no backup. We can't switch those poles around so we pull them apart. We file them down and fit one end into another — what a nightmare! It takes us about nine hours to get this whole thing set up.

"Anyway, we keep reminding ourselves we've got food, water and warmth, so of course we'll be okay. We're three good guys. We have the crew in the Hercules coming back to us and dropping more and more supplies. Then we hear another Hercules has come. So we're okay — that's what we keep telling ourselves.

"Another day dawns exactly the same as the one before: cold and white with gusting winds and blowing snow. We spend it just trying to survive.

"Another day, same as yesterday. We're running out of supplies again because only one bundle makes it close enough for us to go out and get it.

"'We have to ration our food and water,' I say glumly. 'Down to one meal a day each. We'll have to radio for more.'

"The Hercules aircraft crew drops us two more toboggans full of survival gear. And then more. One falls close by — 'great!' I say. The other drops a long way off. The captain tells us they must leave. We thank him for everything and try to remain cheerful. Not long after, a second Hercules, conducting training in the area, is diverted to us to attempt an air supply. The commander is determined to place the precious cargo we need right on the mark. He brings the aircraft down as low as 500 feet above ground in the blizzard. He's flying with instruments, but the spotter at the back can see our position. They drop us three loads, one at a time. The first one we see nothing. The second one is quick flash in the cloud, but we see a parachute overhead for the third … oh, it's landing downwind from us! The plane has exhausted all its supplies but wants to remain overhead as a communication platform.

"We know there are other sleds and drums of supplies out there. One of us has to go out and get at least one of them or we're not going to make it; we'll freeze. We might starve. Who's going to be the one to walk out into the middle of this blizzard?

"'The thing is, it's suicidal to go out alone,' I say to the others. We have to think what to do. Whoever goes out should have a buddy. Brian and I talk about it. If one of us gets in trouble, we've got the other. The problem is that we can't leave Jason alone. We've taken these risks so he won't be by himself. What if something happens to both of us out in the blizzard? — He's back to where he was before — stuck here all by himself. But how many people are you going to throw to the sharks?

"I make a decision. 'Brian, you stay and take care of Jason. I'll go out — I'll be all right. I've got a compass, a radio, and the Herc is up there ...' Then I start thinking: *What if my GPS fails?* I mean, it's an electronic device and its batteries can die. I know I have the Hercules above me ... the

After the Blizzard. SAR Techs Brian Decaire (left) and Darcy St. Laurent (right).

crew can direct me and give me compass bearings if I press the switch and talk. They can figure out where I am and guide me back and forth until I find the camp. Telling myself these things, I go out into the blizzard."

"I tell you, the hairs stand up on the back of my neck when he walks out," Jason says. "I watch him go off the tail of the chopper into the snow where he can't see in front of his nose. He goes a few feet and it's as though he never existed."

"I'm walking, and it's easy because I have the wind at my back," Darcy says. "I walk and walk. Better trust the compass. Suddenly, above the noise of the wind, I hear the distinct sound of the screamers that we put on the supply bundles — holy cow, they work! And then I come upon it — a bright orange toboggan lying upside down in the snow. Now I've got to face directly into the wind and pull all 250 pounds of it back to the chopper. I start back. But I seem to be going in circles, going round and round the camp. My GPS tells me to go left — to go right — to go left. I'm so tired. I've run out of energy. My blood sugar must have dropped since we started rationing supplies. I'll sit down a bit. I drop into the snow and reach into my sleeve where I keep a power gel — the kind marathon runners use. I put it in my cheek, and sit back. Rest a bit. I'll be okay. I start thinking about things, and remember I have another mode on my GPS — the compass mode — but also a map mode. I push a button and it shows me where I've been and where I was; shows me I'm only 150 metres from the camp — *okay!* I jump up and, pulling the toboggan behind me, drag it forward until I see the outline of the helicopter. I get on radio to Brian. — *Please come and help me out!*

"It has taken me over two hours to find a toboggan and haul it back to the helicopter. I've struggled in temperatures of minus 35 degrees and in violent winds that sweep heavy snow at me and over me.

"'Okay fellas, dinner is on me tonight,' I say."

"He comes back with the sled — what a joyous moment," Jason says. "The sled has a beacon, and a siren attached to it, but of course we can't hear the siren because of the wind. We've been worried sick about him all the time he's been out there. Then suddenly he's at the door looking like a crusted-up snowman. Great thing is, he has a sled with him."

Brian cooks up a full meal that evening, and it's devoured in short order.

"The toboggan is full of warm clothes, food, and fuel," Darcy says. "It helps us get through another day. Then what? We look at each other as we listen to a forecast that tells us conditions won't change for the next two days. All of us feel the savage cold and how it bites. It stings. It penetrates through us and is demoralizing: A whole crushing white world that blinds and suffocates us. Feeling discouraged, we keep calling on the satellite phone, desperately hoping to hear that the weather will change; that the blizzard will let up and they can get us out of here."

"But it's great having more food and gear," Brian says. "We try to sleep another night but don't get much. Another day dawns; we can hardly tell it from night because of the blizzard still howling. Winds blow snow thick all around us and high up in the air. I think about the whole psychology of it all and how we don't know if

FASCINATING FACT
The Body's Metabolism in Very Cold Weather

Cold weather drives up the body's metabolism, and it's not unusual for polar explorers to consume up to 7,000 calories each day.

we'll ever get out. Sometimes we've got contact with the outside world, sometimes not. All day we work hard to build up the walls of our camp, but it's very uncomfortable and we're very cold and miserable. Everything flaps and we can't sleep."

"Let's use the helicopter for sleeping," Jason suggests.

"Well, it's not something usually advised," Darcy says. "Without heating in it, moisture will build up and we have to be able to dry our clothes. There's another thing: If you heat it, it becomes a fire hazard. But we'll try it, I mean, what else can we do? We have no other options. We're three frozen men. We take the Coleman lamp and our sleeping bags inside and curl up in our new shelter. What comforts us is knowing that the crew in the Hercules will keep coming with more supplies.

"And they keep coming. Six whole sleds. But we can't see them for the blizzard. Wind blows them far from our small camp and they're lost."

Frustrated, the crew in the Hercules tries dropping two drums instead of the toboggans, thinking they might not so easily go astray. Attached to them are 600 feet of bright yellow rope that trails them, making them a much larger target for the men searching for them in the blizzard. Finding the rope will lead them to the barrel. One thing they know is that if only they can get to some of these supplies, they'll survive.

They retrieve two of the barrels and now have sufficient supply to last a long time. That evening the three eat, and talk about anything and everything to pass the time. Darcy and Brian remain frozen in their clothes. Jason wears Gore-Tex, so he lends one of them his jacket. He listens to the two SAR Techs talk; thinks about all the supplies that have been dropped — already they must have emptied out the Winnipeg hangars and there can't be much left. It is amazing to him — and moving too — how many keep coming, and how hard Search and Rescue try to help them.

"We're cold, uncomfortable and worried," Brian says. "We huddle in the tent to eat, and crawl into the helicopter at night to sleep. It's like we're living in a wind tunnel — dark, noisy and cold. I can't tell you how miserable it is. We're terrified the chopper will roll over in the wind; that before we're rescued we'll suffocate under tons of snow and be dead. We'll be buried in the helicopter anyway, with the way the snow is coming down and piling over the skids — hundreds of feet of it! By the third day we just give up worrying about that.

"Day five dawns; we wake up to see frost glistening on the helicopter windows. Patches of blue sky peep through a white cloud cover. We hear the weather forecast is for fine, clear weather. Immediately I call for a pickup.

"Ken Borek Air, a twin Otter that specializes in flying in the Arctic and other harsh environments, flies in to pick us up. We prepare a makeshift runway for a light plane on skis, then, while waiting, we search for the supply bundles dropped that have gone astray. In one bundle, we find luxury items such as Tim Hortons sandwiches, magazines, candy bars, and newspapers!

"The pilot lands with his skis on the ice, picks us up, and flies us to the camp where Jason has been working at Rankin Inlet. The Hercules crew had sent stretchers for us to sleep on during the journey and the crew cook meals for us."

Darcy and Brian meet Jason's buddies, and Jason hears that when his mates received news that he'd gone down, they prepared themselves to go out on Ski-Doos to try to get him, if no one else would. Then they heard that two SAR Techs jumped in to rescue him.

"What if I'd been left there on my own for five days?" Jason asks afterwards. "What would have happened to me? Oh yeah, I was scared and I did shed a few tears. But those guys took care of me. I tell you, I was frightened. I can survive anywhere in an area where there is a tree line — just give me trees — but this environment gave no relief — nothing! I can run around in treed areas and minus 30 degree temperatures, but this, I mean, there was nowhere to hide …

"I can't say enough about the Military — they sacrificed for me and I'm just a small pea in a pod. Those SAR Techs, they were a class act. They were scared out of their minds but they didn't show it. They didn't know me from a hole in the ground. They just knew they had a guy in trouble, and they risked their own lives to come in and save me. When Darcy went out to find the sled of supplies, he walked into an abyss. That, to me, just made the hairs on the back of my neck stand up because at one point I was scared to get out of the helicopter, afraid I wasn't going to find my way back. He just got out there with the compass, the GPS, found it, and dragged it back through the wind and the snow. It took everything he had to get it back.

"I've been around choppers and pilots all my life. I've been a pilot for Search and Rescue; done lots of training. I've swung people off roofs of houses — all a part of my life: Then this. Yes, I saw the mistakes I made — like I should have looked at the weather more closely. But I've had no nightmares and I've chosen not to be traumatized. How could I be? Those guys who came to help me, that's what I remember. They are incredible — a class act. They are very professional and make sacrifices all the time. They were so on top of things it was impressive — I've never seen anything like it. To me, they are true heroes."

Jason was born in northern Alberta, the son of a commercial pilot. As a youngster, he saw a lot of helicopter activity, watched them flying overhead, and eventually they became a familiar part of his life growing up.

"This genre of flying is the technical side of helicopters," he says. "You get used to remote areas, for this is where most of the work is. I've never had a bad experience, just mechanical failures, that's all."

Sometime after his rescue, a pilot from Jason's company flew down to dig out his helicopter. He is still flying it.

"Why do I do scary work like this?" Darcy St. Laurent tells how he first joined the Army and spent 20 years there.

"My dreams of doing this kind of work began when I was a child listening to my older brothers, my dad, and my uncles talk about their adventures," he says. "From watching documentaries about daring adventures and rescues, I saw SAR Technicians parachuting in to rescue the people who were stranded and decided I wanted to do that kind of thing. It was interesting and cool. It was neat to help people and live epic adventures. I guess you have to be careful what you dream for; it may actually happen.

"I became a combat engineer and went as a soldier to Bosnia. Then to Cambodia as part of a United Nations mission. After I trained as a Search and Rescue Technician I was stationed first in Greenwood, Nova Scotia, and now I'm in Winnipeg.

"I have to say I'm a hard worker; I've trained for many winter outdoor sports such as biathlons, am a strong skier and snowshoer, and have experience in outdoor adventurous sports — so you could say I'm suited to this work. At present I am planning an expedition from Ellesmere Island to the North Pole.

"About this mission: I was relatively experienced, but Search and Rescue Technicians don't often get to jump into conditions like these. You're lucky — or unlucky — to get one in your whole career."

Darcy St. Laurent and Brian Decaire felt honoured to be awarded the Medal of Bravery for this rescue. They have also received recognition for previous rescues: The Chief of the Defence Staff Commendation for parachuting at night into a blizzard to the Pauingassi First Nation. Once there, they treated the victim of a stabbing incident.

Darcy has also been awarded the Star of Courage for a rescue in which he participated in 1998 in Labrador.

2 Mystery of a Disappearing Couple

Vancouver, 1994

It's August 10, and busy as usual at Trader Vic's upscale Polynesian restaurant in North Vancouver. Manager Tommy Chang picks up the phone, makes a note, and hangs up. The following afternoon he places a reserved sign on a table with a view overlooking Coal Harbour and the North Shore mountains. The booking is for Nick Masee, his wife, and an unknown couple.

An hour later, Nick calls to say he will be delayed. Time passes, and more time, but the window seat at Trader Vic's sits empty. The hours tick by and no one arrives.

Another hour passes and Tommy gives the table away. He's surprised at the no-show, because when Nick makes a reservation, he's always punctual.

Since that night, Nick Masee and his wife Lisa have never been seen again. For months afterwards, there is talk of little else but the mystery of the banker and his wife who never kept a date; of a couple who did a disappearing act from the face of the earth.

Questions swirl: Have they been kidnapped? Perhaps they've run off because of money they owed, or because of a bad deal. Are they in a police protection program? Are they alive and enjoying themselves somewhere? — Or are they dead?

|||||||||||||||||||

Nick Masee is a man hooked on the high life, of being seen and counted among the city's wealthy. He loves to dress up in black-tie for dinners at upscale clubs and to accompany clients on weekend trips to exclusive lodges. He enjoys sailing on luxury yachts, and being seen among celebrities at the Hyatt Regency Hotel. Something else: He craves to be among the big players at the Vancouver Stock Exchange.

To casual appearance, his life seems one of considerable affluence: He's on the tennis courts at the West Vancouver Tennis Club; in his swimming pool; at the ballet. He's dining in expensive Robson Street restaurants. His official office might be at the Bank of Montreal on the ninth floor of Bentall 111, but his unofficial digs are on Howe Street. It is here he consorts with some of the city's biggest stockbrokers and promoters, and with rich and influential people.

The reality is otherwise. Although he owns a house with a swimming pool in an upscale area of North Vancouver, although he can choose what pair of designer slacks he will wear from a closet full of them, he can't really afford this life — in fact, he doesn't even have the financial means to eat at Trader Vic's. Money is always on his mind. He never has enough of it and he's in debt. His financial situation might even be considered desperate.

After 37 years, Nick quits his job as private banker to wealthy clients at the Bank of Montreal. He gives it up to act as the marketing face of a company called Turbodyne that manufactures clean air equipment for diesel engines. His job is to find new investors for it. Before the dinner meeting scheduled to take place at Trader Vic's on that fateful night, and the reason for it in the first place, is that Nick has been contacted by someone unknown to him, a stranger who says he has ten million dollars he might be willing to invest in Turbodyne. He suggests they dine at Trader Vic's restaurant to discuss it, and names a date. An hour before the scheduled meeting he phones Nick.

"I'm bringing my wife — why don't you invite yours? I'll send a limousine to pick both of you up."

Nick calls Lisa to tell her.

"This guy has ten million dollars to invest?" Lisa expresses surprise to her colleagues at the hair salon where she works. "And he doesn't know what to do with it? — pretty weird."

Neither Nick and Lisa, nor the investor and his wife, show up that night. Next morning, Lisa calls the hair salon to tell them she'll be away for a few days and says something about a court case. She then calls Nick's workplace to tell them the same thing.

Leon Nowek, a fellow director at Turbodyne, is surprised at Lisa's phone message, surprised that she has phoned, and not Nick. This hasn't happened before. He calls the Masee house half an hour after receiving the message, but gets no answer.

A week passes. Lisa remains absent from her hair salon. No one hears from Nick.

Concerned that she hasn't heard from her sister Lisa for more than a week, Loretta Mo Kuen Leung drops by the Masee house to see what's up. She drives slowly along a residential street in an upscale area of North Vancouver. The air is sultry on this warm August day, but windows of many of the elegant homes are closed, their owners away. Except for an occasional *woof*, and a cat strolling across the hot asphalt, the street is sleepily quiet.

Loretta's first surprise is to see the couple's Chrysler Le Baron in the Masee driveway. Another is to find the front door unlocked and the security system switched off. She looks around, a little uneasy now, but doesn't see any sign of a forced entry. Slowly she pushes open the door. Spider, the family's aging Persian cat, meows loudly as he sidles up to her. He's hungry and unfed. Loretta calls out as she walks through the house.

What's this? In the kitchen, dirty dishes sit piled in the sink. Oh! — Not like Lisa at all. The bedroom door is wide open and the bed unmade. Loretta spots the couple's passports on a bedside table. She picks them up, puts them down, and looks about for other clues to tell her what could possibly have happened; where they might have gone.

As she walks back through the hall she finds three pieces of plastic electrical tapes of the kind that police use as temporary handcuffs. Have Nick and Lisa been forcefully taken from their home? Did they have to leave in a hurry?

Alarmed now, Loretta phones Nick's son and daughter from his first marriage: Nick Junior, who lives in Singapore, and Tanya Van Ravenzwaaij-Masee in the Netherlands. Nick Junior at once makes plans to fly home. Loretta begins asking questions around the neighbourhood.

She contacts all Nick and Lisa's friends and acquaintances.

Nobody has heard a thing. No one knows anything, except for one acquaintance who said he thought he saw them dressed casually and eating hamburgers at a fast food restaurant on the night they were supposed to meet the wealthy investor at Trader Vic's.

Loretta files a missing persons report with the police department.

The police begin their investigations by compiling a profile of Nick and Lisa Masee. First there is a physical description: Nick Masee is a white man aged 56. He is five foot seven in height and 162 pounds. He has wavy grey hair and a moustache. He speaks both English and Dutch. Lisa is an Asian woman aged 39. She is five foot six in height, 111 pounds. She has long black hair, brown eyes, and a slender build. She speaks English and Mandarin, and works six days a week as a hairdresser for a Vancouver hair salon.

Officers gather up all the information they can get about the Masees, beginning with neighbours and friends. The street comes alive with chatter and rumour. The police learn that Nick is a neat and organized man, and scrupulous about his home security.

"He would never have left the house alarm switched off!" one neighbour exclaims.

"He's good to his friends and keeps in close contact with his neighbours," another comments. "But they don't often invite us over because they like to entertain at fancy downtown restaurants."

From all the local comments, police get a picture of a nice, quiet, happily married couple who don't appear to have any problems — not a single enemy in the world, as one neighbour says. They would have told family and friends if they planned to be away and it is totally out of character for them to just disappear. Another thing: Nick would never leave Spider alone with no one to look after him.

"Lisa said she'd come over when my wedding dress was being fitted," says a friend. "So obviously she didn't plan to be gone — anyway, she would have called."

Loretta learns that Nick is on the Board of Directors of Ballet BC and regularly organized fundraising events for it. She approaches the general manager.

"Yes, Nick worked for us," Howard Jang says. "He was supposed to attend a board meeting on August 23, but didn't show up — not like him."

The police hear so many comments about the couple's plans to attend various local events in the weeks after their disappearance that it seems to them unlikely they would have just gone off on a holiday. Besides, no one knew of travel arrangements they might have made. They speak to Nick's son, Nick Junior, who had flown in from Singapore on hearing the news of the disappearances. The younger Nick recounts how he'd spoken to his father a few days before he disappeared.

"He never mentioned he would be going away, either for vacation or pleasure," he says. But it is when Nick's daughter Tanya Van Ravenzwaaij-Masee from the Netherlands speaks up that further clouds begin to gather.

"My father called me earlier this year — in April," Tanya says. "He told me he'd be out of town on my birthday and wouldn't be able to call. This is completely out of character for him because he always told me where he'd be. I swear he was acting strangely before his disappearance. He'd become a bit secretive about his life, and also about his work — not like him at all. He always enjoyed sharing details of his life with others; he was always an open man. When I heard him say he felt concerned for his safety I called my brother to tell him about the conversation."

Concerned, Nick Junior had phoned his father. "I was very troubled by his mentioning the possibility of something bad happening to him and Lisa," he tells police, and the investigating team turns to Nick's business life to begin interviewing old Bank associates and business partners.

A spokesperson for the Bank of Montreal declines to make a comment on the bank's behalf. But others speak up.

"Nick Masee would never get mixed up in something shady," Murray Pezim, one of Nick's richest clients, says. "He was my banker when he was head of private banking. I'm worried about him. Something's definitely wrong. I can't see him getting involved in anything. He was a quiet guy, not a promoter type or anything like that."

A friend and colleague mentions that he spoke with Nick just about every day and knew about the potential investor. When Nick didn't show up, the friend supposed that he'd gone to California where Turbodyne headquarters is located, together with the stranger who had ten million dollars.

Don Hannah is a management consultant and financial investor who lives across the street from the Masees. Earlier he had expressed his great surprise that Nick had left his front door open, and that he'd abandoned his beloved cat Spider — "because they looked after him very well," he says, and adds that it is also surprising the car had been left in the driveway.

"If there is something foul," he says, "it's related to the Vancouver Stock Exchange. If it's not that, then the guy is taking a holiday or something."

On the theme of money, another neighbour said, "Nick dealt with people who were wealthy, as opposed to himself in the salaried class. He was in pretty big company on a modest budget."

During the investigations, Nick Junior remains living in the Masee house, trying to piece together details of his father's recent life. It is a solitary existence for him with only Spider for company, a cat who might be the only creature to know what had actually happened in the house. Eventually Nick moves the contents of the home into storage for safekeeping and returns to Singapore. But he does begin his own investigation and, like the police, quickly draws nothing but blanks.

"There's no clue or hint as to anything," he says in frustration.

Eventually, puzzling details begin to emerge, all related to money and the Vancouver Stock Exchange. First there is Nick's association with Fred Hofman, a fellow Dutchman who disappeared in 1991 leaving behind ten million dollars in debts and the shattered lives of many elderly victims who had trusted him with their money. A Canada-wide warrant still exists for his arrest for theft and fraud. Nick had introduced some of these victims to the fugitive Hofman. In particular a Doctor Quentin Johnson who lost two to three million dollars to him, and who also seems to have disappeared.

"Nick looked up to Fred Hofman as a Dutchman who had been around longer," an associate says. "And [because] he had a reputation with the Vancouver Stock Exchange."

Others argue there is no evidence to connect the two, even though both are Dutch and grew up close to each other in their home country. Hofman has not been seen for three years — *another disappearing Dutchman* — but there is no reason to believe Nick has joined him in hiding.

North Vancouver Sergeant Jack Ewart and Constable John Chersak begin working full-time on the file. With what they have found, they really have no starting point for their investigation, and nothing to go on. They have not been able to find the limousine or taxi, the investor with the ten million dollars — or anything else.

"It's early in the game, but there is a degree of frustration to it," Sergeant Ewart says. "We have no real starting point. We're tracking shadows. We are classifying it as a suspicious missing persons case, but we have to keep an open mind. There is no evidence of kidnapping but it's getting more suspicious as time progresses and publicity expands."

Speculation is endless. Police believe there is more to the story than meets the eye. Nick and Lisa Masee are probably dead, victims of foul play. But it's possible they are in a protection program.

Nick Junior offers a reward of $25,000 to anyone who can come up with information leading to the whereabouts of his father and stepmother. "Somebody out there knows something," he says. He has a poster made up to announce it, and adds: *Foul play is strongly suspected in their disappearance.* He also hires Ozzie Kaban, a well-known private detective, to investigate.

Kaban becomes suspicious of the story about the Masees who were to have met with an investor at Trader Vic's. Especially since a contact reported he'd seen the two, dressed casually and eating hamburgers in Bayshore that same night. Not exactly the way you'd meet a big investor, he thinks. Eventually he travels to the Cayman Islands in pursuit of leads. There he locates some of Nick's money. He learns the two enjoyed time there for both business dealings and pleasure. A contact tells him Nick and Lisa had taken a trip to the Islands in April of 1994 without telling anyone. *Evidence that they did not always inform family or friends of their movements.* Once there, they had opened up a bank account and had wills drawn up.

"Note that Nick is not wanted in any criminal investigation," the private detective says. He adds that he suspects, like others do, that Nick had some involvement with Fred Hofman.

Kaban long continues to believe the Masees are still alive. Late in 1994 he hits a dead end. With all the information he has, he concludes the couple must be living in Belize, the South American country often mentioned in connection with Hofman.

"I wouldn't be surprised if they are sharing the same bit of beach," Kaban says. "I could be wrong, but I don't think [they] are dead. People just don't disappear."

Vancouver's business community and its Stock Exchange still rocks with rumours: The Masees got involved in money laundering for the Hells Angels motorcycle gang. They took several million dollars of their drug money and either fled with it, or were abducted. Afterwards their kidnappers tried to extort the money back from them. Nick Masee helped put together an illegal arms deal worth a hundred million dollars. He had contacts in Libya, Iraq, and Vietnam. He was killed because he had too much knowledge of the deal. Others insist he was kidnapped because of gambling debts run up by a major player on the Vancouver Stock Exchange.

"Bad debts — that's what their disappearance is about," Adrian du Plessis, a Howe Street insider, comments.

The police state these are just rumours. There was no doubt Nick enjoyed rubbing shoulders with people in high circles, that he had dealings with questionable characters. But there was much to show he was an honest and decent man.

"Straight as an arrow, that's what he was," Capozzi, a former client says. "The kind of guy who, if he won money at a poker game, he'd declare it on his income tax — there are no dark sides."

"Considering who Nick dealt with, it's a miracle his accounts were so clean," a lawyer says of him.

"My father was very money- and status-conscious," Nick Junior says. "But he wasn't a rich man. When he went to Trader Vic's he used a discount two-for-one card."

"He enjoyed the Howe Street life," Murray Pezim comments. "He knew everything about the street, but had no street smarts. Number one, this is about money. He got himself into the wrong place at the wrong time."

In 2001, seven years after the disappearance of Nick and Lisa Masee, Nick's son and daughter apply to the Supreme Court of British Columbia to have their parents declared legally dead. Lisa's sister Loretta Mo Kuen Leung joins in a petition that includes the statement, "Death is the only reasonable conclusion."

Homicide detectives understand that people need closure. Families need to know where a missing member is and what happened to them. Most of all: Are they alive and will they come walking in the door one day, even 15 years later? Or are they dead? Police must determine if there has been any criminal activity; has there been murder? Crime, and particularly murder, should not go unpunished.

The Masee case is 14 years old, and police are still holding out hope that somebody remembers something about the fate of the North Vancouver couple who vanished. On an anniversary of the couple's disappearance, once again they circulate descriptions of the two in the hope of cracking the case.

"We're patient. We never give up," Corporal Murray Watt says. "We know it's possible that the bad guy might decide at some point to confide in someone — maybe a girlfriend. People like to talk — to get things off their chests and confess. The person they confided in sometimes gets a guilty conscience. It's possible that after 30 years they no longer feel afraid of that person and persuade themselves they should just go to the police and tell what they know. A man might walk into a detachment and say, 'I've got information about something that happened 30 years ago.'

"Sometimes that's all we need," Watt says. "We'll go to the media, even if it's 20 years later. We'll say, 'look, we don't forget these things. We've got a possible murder file but we still don't know what happened. We're looking for tips from the public.' We review a case again and again to try to move it forward. A murder file is always in the queue, and stays open until all possibilities are gone. This might be when a murderer is 80 years old, or so old he can't be alive any more. Then we close it."

"Sometimes a criminal doesn't know I'm coming," he says. "They think they got away with what they did; that we've forgotten. Sometimes they get careless. We know there are people out there who have information about the Masees. With large files like this one, some things happen at the [crime] scene that only the investigators and the criminals know about: particular things we might find — like the firing of a type or calibre of bullet used; things done to a body afterwards; objects left at the scene. We hold that information back so the bad guy does not know what we've learned.

"I have information about the Masee file that only the murderers have," he adds. "The public doesn't know. Sometimes there is nothing that can be done with this unless we get a confession. When we question a suspect, he might let something slip that only he knows, or that we, the police, know. When confronted, he'll say something like, 'well, I didn't know that … I read it in the paper … I heard someone say it.' This is impossible because nobody else knew it."

"All crime is about robbing," he adds. "Robbing someone of their possessions, of their identity; you are taking something from somebody. The Masees were probably murdered. Murder is the ultimate crime, the very worst thing you can do. You are robbing someone of their very life. It should not go unpunished." He pauses, then adds, "The Biblical *thou shalt not kill,* actually reads in the original Hebrew translation as *thou shalt not murder.*"

Murray Watt, like many of his counterparts in the RCMP, is a quiet hero. He is patient, diligent, and painstaking. If someone has murdered the Masees, he will never quit his hunt for the person or persons who did it. He'll walk into a cold case and flip the lids of infinite numbers of boxes. Patiently he'll go through their files. He'll ask himself: Where can we take this with what we've got — with new investigative techniques? Has the law changed so we can now do a different type of surveillance? Should we try a wiretap? — If so, I'll have to write out a warrant and affidavit to the judge. I want to go through it all again. Take it back to the public. Issue a press release to say that the police are still looking for tips on the case. If anyone knows anything, if anyone feels guilty, please come forward. Help us out.

"It could trigger something — like the guy who was afraid to come to us when we first went public. *Nick Masee told me who he was going to meet that night. I was afraid the fellow would come after me, but it's a long time now …*"

Corporal Watt takes up paper, and piece by piece, painstakingly begins the process of creating a new narrative of the case — a chronological account of what happened, the date when it happened, who did this, and who did that. Hey, we should try this, we should try that; see if it works. For this process he uses a TIP system.

"It's a huge amount of paper to deal with," he says. "Sometimes — in this case when the couple's son and daughter ask the court to declare their parents dead — an officer has to summarize the contents of ten or more boxes of files and make a presentation to a judge. This type of reporting is a skill; it's an art to condense large volumes of information. And it must be presented in a coherent and readable manner.

"In fact, many of the jobs we perform are essentially about

> ## FASCINATING FACT
> ### The TIP System
>
> The TIP System is used to organize and itemize all information collected about a case. Examples, not necessarily in order, are:
>
> TIP No. 1: Table of contents.
> TIP No. 2: All reports that go to a division.
> TIP No. 3: Exhibit reports.
> TIP No. 4: Lab reports.
> TIP No. 5: Press releases.
> TIP No. 6: Profiles of victim, of the suspect/s.
> TIP No. 7: Coroners report.
> TIP No. 8: Interview.
>
> Some files contain 500 TIPs. Watt cross-references them all. Somebody reads through them to see that the investigation is being properly handled.

investigation, then report writing," he says, and repeats that it's a huge skill to be able to articulate what you've done and present it well. Indeed, his own ability to synthesize large volumes of information and write up excellent reports is known among his colleagues at the Force. Corporal Watt explains how it came about, and why he took up police work.

"I spent four years in university studying forestry," he said. "When I learned that the work would be seasonal, I went back to university for another four years to study geology — I enjoyed life in the back-country and in remote places — but when I graduated and went to look for work, the jobs were not there. The economy had died. What was I going to do now?"

With influence from an OPP officer and family friend, Murray Watt walked into the Thunder Bay RCMP police detachment one day to apply to enter the Force.

"It's not unusual not to start out in the direction you end up in," he says. "I looked at policing and thought, *this is something I could be interested in*. It grew on me, and I saw that it wasn't a lot different from forestry, or from geology and my science background. Both were about investigating and writing reports. I saw that it is similar to what a policeman does:

He or she takes pieces of information, talks to people, and puts it into a collection. When I was a geologist walking through the bush, I came across a rock. I looked at it as mineralogy that could give me a piece of information, for example, the rock folds. I'd come to the next outcrop and study it to get information. I would project what went on in between — all of that is about investigating. And then writing reports.

"In the same way, police take statements from people. They deal with forensic evidence, fingerprints, and different pieces of information. They then put them together and write a report. Paperwork is the biggest part of the job.

"Policing is a great job," he says. "There's camaraderie, bonding with people that you go through difficult or unusual circumstances with. And you never stop learning. Out of 12 months of the work year, you're on courses for two. Some have to be regularly upgraded because you can gradually lose these skills if you don't use them. Not only that, but new and different techniques can come up for dealing with violence. Then sometimes the rules change. For me, a management course might come up. Or a riot squad tactical team course where I'll learn how to drive a city bus if needed. Another thing: the RCMP is so big you can always do something different.

"About the Masees and their disappearance, we referred this case to our Serious Crime and Homicide Division," he says. "Serious Crime goes after assaults, assaults with weapons, and vicious attacks — incidents like that. We also have an integrated homicide investigation team that is created from police forces from all over British Columbia, with the exception of Delta, Vancouver, and West Vancouver. It includes federal, provincial, and municipal police — a specialty group of investigators who go after a homicide.

"We know the Masees are not in hiding. They paid the price for getting involved with organized crime. Either they were complacent,

---

FASCINATING FACT
Courses That Must Be Upgraded:

• Shooting skills and firearms qualifications.
• Human rights issues such as a harassment investigator's course.
• Crime investigation techniques.
• Undercover operations.
• How to use evidence to better interrogate people.
• Self-defence and how to fight to win.
• First-aid.
• Traffic control.

or wilfully blind, but they still got caught up in things they shouldn't have. Organized crime is only about money, and you have to know how to hide it. Nick was a banker, and he would know.

"Whatever happened to that couple, we will not give up. We'll find the persons responsible for their disappearance. I might have to track down people who have fled the country. If I do, I'll go through Interpol. It will check another country's constitution to see how samples can be collected, how people can be interrogated, and what rights a suspect has there. Each country is different and I have to know what I can do and not do.

FASCINATING FACT
Interpol

The International Criminal Police Organization known as Interpol fosters international police co-operation. It was established as the International Criminal Police Commission in 1923 and adopted its telegraphic address as its name in 1956. It should not be confused with the International Police, which takes on an active uniformed role in policing war-torn countries.

Interpol's role is to assist national police forces in identifying and/or locating suspected criminals with a view to their arrest and extradition.

It is the world's fifth-largest international organization with 186 countries as members. It provides finance of around US$59 million through annual contributions made by the member nations. Its headquarters are in Lyon, France.

As an organization it strives to remain politically neutral. Its constitution forbids it to become involved in crimes that do not overlap several member countries, or in any political, military, religious, or racial crimes. It focuses particularly on public safety, terrorism, organized crime, illicit drug production, drug trafficking, weapons smuggling, human trafficking, money laundering, white-collar crime, computer crime, intellectual property crime, and corruption.

"I'll go through the Masee file, or one that's 20 years old," he says. "I'll get to the Exhibit Tip and look through the hard evidence collected all those years ago to see if there is anything useful for DNA testing. Then I'll write up a report."

What he does is out of the spotlight and generally not appreciated by the public. His work might not seem dramatic — like busting a drug ring or arresting a suspect at a high-profile crime scene. None of it can compete in the popular imagination with the romantic origins of the RCMP — the North-West Mounted Police — and its legendary tales of 140 years ago. Our officer is a hero of a kind quite different from an RCMP predecessor like Sir Sam Steele. But he, and all officers like him and the work they do, should not be forgotten.

Courtesy of the National Film Board of Canada, Toronto Reference Library Archives.

RCMP officers in signature red coats and black pants: to the right is a commanding officer with beret and sword and to the left is an officer.

A Flight Back into 1886

Sir Sam puts a machine gun down on the path to the Yukon to bar Americans from entering because they allow lynching and shooting on their side. He wants them to understand that this is Canadian territory. Also, he doesn't want to use force to subdue all the hundreds of unruly prospectors rushing to the Yukon to strike gold. Or to look after them once they get there.

"No one will be allowed to enter the Yukon without a ton of goods to support themselves," he decrees. In this way he prevents desperate speculators and adventurers from entering Canada and creating havoc.

During this period, Steele and the North-West Mounted Police made the Klondike gold rush one of the most orderly of its kind in history and the Mounted Police famous all over the world. Tales of their heroic deeds have yet to fade in the yellowed pages of old history books; these were the glory days for a Force now known as the RCMP.

The RCMP has a colourful history. It began as the North-West Mounted Police (NWMP), originally created in 1873 to establish law and order in the Canadian West. Sir John A. Macdonald, the prime minister at the time, felt alarmed by the lawlessness caused by whiskey traders in southern Alberta. He ordered the Force to Fort Whoop-up (near present-day Lethbridge) in 1874, to put a stop to it.

In 1886, he sent the North-West Mounted Police to Fortymile River country near the Alaska–Yukon Territory when a rich gold strike set off a stampede of gold seekers. The government wanted to protect the Native people from liquor traders. To keep some form of order so that major commercial interests were protected. Not least, to make sure the area remained Canadian. The first actual Mounted Police post in the Yukon was built at Fortymile and named after Charles Constantine, its first superintendent. Just 19 men were first sent, although Constantine had asked for "a force of 50 experienced and sober men of large and powerful builds."

By 1896, the NWMP had been established as the only legitimate authority in the Yukon. Inspector Constantine acted as customs officer, postmaster, Indian agent, land agent, and justice of the peace, as well as registering miners' claims. It was he who established the foundation of Canadian law and authority in this huge northern frontier during the tough times of the Klondike gold rush.

Courtesy of the Canadian Pacific Railway, Toronto Reference Library Archives.

Portrait of Superintendent Samuel B. Steele of the North-West Mounted Police.

FASCINATING FACT
Miner's Outfit

A one-year outfit for a miner consisted of a list of goods that was said to weigh one ton and cost about $2,000. It included hundreds of pounds of food; cooking pots, utensils, cups and plates, gold pan, axes, picks and other tools, canvas tent, blankets, candles, soap, lamps and lamp oil, and two or more sets of clothing — from woolen socks and boots to mittens and hats.

The gold rush began in 1896 with a strike at Rabbit Creek, and a stampede followed the discovery. In 1897, when news of the strike reached the outside world, a rush truly got started. From the fall of 1897 through 1898, tens of thousands of gold seekers headed for the Klondike fields, most entering Canada at Chilkoot Pass and White Pass summits. The Force in the Yukon swelled from 19 men in 1896 to 285 men by November 1898.

Samuel Steele replaced Constantine in 1898. He arrived at the foot of Chilkoot Pass in February to find thousands of men waiting to pack their supplies over the pass. He immediately stationed permanent police detachments at the summits of Chilkoot and White passes, both to keep law and order, and to establish Canadian sovereignty at these two international borders.

The remoteness of the Klondike goldfields, as well as the scarcity and high cost of food and supplies in Dawson City, created desperate conditions for many men arriving in the North. This is when Steele established the rule that gold seekers coming into the Yukon bring with them a minimum amount of provisions. The North-West Mounted Police enforced it because chaos must be prevented.

The North-West Mounted Police were given the title "Royal" by the British government in 1904 in recognition of their outstanding service to Canada. In 1920, they became the Royal Canadian Mounted Police.

The Mounted Police continued to play a memorable role in the development of the Yukon. In the 1940s, the RCMP took over patrolling the newly built Alaska Highway. It sent detachments to Whitehorse, Haines Junction, Teslin, and Watson Lake, and others to man three traffic control gates.

From the beginning, the NWMP captured the public's imagination. Tales of their triumphs and tragedies in bringing law and order to the Far North were given a lot of publicity in

Courtesy of the National Film Board of Canada, Toronto Reference Library Archives.

The RCMP has a proud history, dating back to 1873 when the Force was known as the North-West Mounted Police.

North America and helped to create the popular image of the "determined, dauntless, and incorruptible Mountie."

The distinctive red uniform associated with the RCMP is now worn only at formal occasions. Its predecessor, the Service Order of Dress, was worn in 1897 at Queen Victoria's Diamond Jubilee. Its appearance left a distinct impression on London: the red cloth tunic, white gauntlets, blue breeches, black boots, Model 76 Winchester rifle and broad-brimmed

FASCINATING FACT
Sir Sam Steele: An Early Hero of the NWMP

Sir Sam Steele had a reputation for an incredible 19 hours a day at summit crossings. His mission was to make sure that the Canadian system of justice was upheld. In 1871 he joined the military. By 1873 he became only the third officer to be sworn in to the newly created North-West Mounted Police. He was given the title of staff constable. He was wanted because of his excellent horsemanship, his skills as a "man-at-arms" — and for his ability to drill new recruits!

Sam was present at the second rebellion of Louis Riel. He was asked to try to negotiate with Sitting Bull after he defeated General Custer at the Battle of Little Bighorn. Sitting Bull had fled to Canada with his people to escape American revenge. Sam's job was to persuade Sitting Bull to go back to the United States. But Sitting Bull would not be persuaded. He said he wanted to live under Queen Victoria. Sam said, "Okay, as long as you obey the law."

Later, Sam was sent to the site of the North-West Rebellion to fight against Big Bear's last rebel force. At Loon Lake, in the final battle on Canadian territory, Sam led his Mounties to victory over Big Bear's forces.

But this was not enough: Sam wanted more recognition. He wanted titles and more authority. So he travelled up to Dawson, taking with him the author Jack London. Once there, he told him to write down everything that he said. The author was to come up with ideas for slogans so that Sam could impress the queen and be given a knighthood. He would then become a hero and be forever remembered inside the pages of the history books.

He is described in the Barks/Rosa stories in *Hearts of the Yukon*: "[Sam Steele] moved to Dawson City in 1898. Apparently the citizens were both impressed and scared at his coming. On his arrival he makes a speech that includes his whole life story and everything he has accomplished.

"Pretentious, someone mutters, and glittering Goldie O'Gilt denounces him for making her work for him, although it seems this was her punishment for trying to steal his gold nugget."

felt hat exemplified for many the dash, romance, and courage for which the North-West Mounted Police were known.

Today, the RCMP is at once a national, provincial, and local police force. It polices from the Prairies, Rocky Mountains, up to the high Arctic, across remote parts of provinces and throughout cities. Officers walk and ride bicycles. They use trained dogs, ride on horses, in planes, and on snowmobiles. Seldom do we see the striking scarlet uniform, and too often the organization and its officers receive bad press because one lone officer messes up. This is a pity. An RCMP officer involved in local general city policing in one day might respond to eight to ten calls.

"I'm in my car," Corporal Watt says. "I get a call to deal with a disturbance somewhere; then a next-of-kin notification. I do the paperwork, get back in my car, and go to the next call, which could be bullying in school. A domestic abuse scene might come up where I'll go to the home of a man who is beating up his wife and she's suffered a serious injury. I subdue the fellow and charge him with assault. I think I've helped the wife. Next day she denies he touched her and won't press charges.

"You've lived through all these experiences; through other people's emotions vicariously. It's tough. People swear at you and give you the finger. You suffer when one officer screws up because in the public mind, the whole Force has screwed up. All of this does things to you, but the trick is not to take it home. You need to talk over with someone what you've been through — it helps get rid of what's inside. If you have a serious incident — or anything that bugs you — you have to talk. You have to have a debriefing and get the two sides of your brain to talk to each other. You can't lock it inside."

Unlike his predecessor, Sir Sam Steele, Murray Watt, in 2008, is not chasing mad trappers, whiskey traders, or running outlaws. But he is after people who commit serious crimes. He — and all homicide investigators — will never give up.

"About the Masees and their disappearance," he continues. "It's always about how much manpower, how many officers do you give to a particular investigation. It takes officers away from other cases. It's always a balance: Our people are not dedicated to one case, but work on many. The current level of investigators was set in 2005 at 84, plus support staff.

"It's 14 years, and the Masee file is still open. I'm not giving up. Someone out there knows something. Crime will not go unpunished."

At the time of writing, Murray Watt, when not engaged in current duties, still patiently investigates endless boxes of cold case files, always on a hunt for something — anything — that might have been overlooked.

3 To Fall Off a Mountain

Two young men make a spur-of-the-moment decision to go climbing — all the way to the top of Mount Dione, high in the ranges north of Vancouver. James Campbell and Mick Littleton (not their real names) have many years of climbing experience and each has dreamed of conquering these particular peaks. Most people don't even think of trying. It's already September and the weather forecast is for warm, sunny days ahead. Mick would never confess it, but sometimes in his dreams he hears the mountains whisper: *Come on up, come on up.*

The two men head for Squamish, a picturesque little town perched at the edge of the Sea-to-Sky Highway between Vancouver and Whistler. It is a famous destination for climbers from all over the world.

Each man scrambles to get ready before setting off for the climb. Their plan is to take a technical route and scale alpine rock, all the way to the summit of Mount Dione above the tree line. They will camp out at the top, and then leave the next day for the long and difficult trek to Lake Lovelywater. The day after, they'll rendezvous with the helicopter pilot. For this ambitious climb they'll need rope, an ice axe, crampons, rock and ice gear — as well as all their skill and experience.

On September 17, the two men climb aboard a chartered helicopter that will fly them to the spot where they will begin their climb. Mick presses his thin face to the window and stares at Mount Stawamus, crowning jewel of all the mountain ranges. It stands alone in the sunshine at the head of Howe Sound. He looks at it in awe. A climber can choose among more than 400 routes, all of them long, free climbs to the top, and the only places in North America where people can scale such spectacular granite walls — aside from the infamous towers of Yosemite of course.

Today, the views from the helicopter are picture-perfect: old forests, endless mountain ranges, and impressive waterfalls, with Chief Stawumus at the heart of it all. The sky is cobalt blue. Under a brilliant sun, a line of footprints is seen tracking up to a windless summit. It is a climber's paradise.

The helicopter pilot hovers over a lonely snow-capped crest as he searches for a spot to land. He finds one, and the two men drop down into the snow with all their equipment. They will begin their climb right here.

"See you at the pickup spot at Lake Lovelywater, day after next," calls the pilot as he spins his blades for takeoff.

The two leave their gear at Red Tit Hut on the *col*, or small pass, between the Serratus and Dione mountain peaks, then set out to climb the route up Mount Dione — all 6,700 feet of it. The air feels warm and mellow. Sunrays glance off the granite walls and dance over remnants of old winter snow. James's mind soars, but he notices that Mick seems preoccupied.

The two climb all day, reaching the summit by nightfall. This first night is spent on a ledge partly sheltered by an overhanging rocky lip. The night temperature dips and a chill wind blows from the north. Both men are a bit the worse for wear in the morning, particularly Mick, who has forgotten to bring all his water and feels a bit dehydrated because of it.

James glances at his partner. He looks tired, his eyes a little bloodshot. His movements are slow. Well, they are up here now; he'll just have to keep an eye on him.

The two prepare for a series of rappels down vertical rock. This will bring them to glaciated snow below — hard snow that never melts because it's forever hidden from the sun in north-facing valleys. Each man ties a long rope to an anchor. With it they will climb down to the next

FASCINATING FACT
A Rock Climber's Dictionary

Mushrooms — so called because of the shape of the platform. In this case, the bridge consisted of unsupported snow.

Bergschrund — a crevasse or gap at the junction of a steep upper slope with a glacier or névé where the top of the glacier pulls away from the rock face.

Névé — an expanse of granular snow on the upper part of a glacier that has not yet been compressed into ice.

station. Before moving on, they pull the rope through its anchor; they'll take it with them and use it again.

"We prefer to make use of natural anchors if any are available," James says. "You look for a rocky horn protrusion, or an ice bollard tree trunk. But — no trees up here so that's no option."

James comes down the last part — about 100 feet — and lands on a bridged ice mushroom that is supported over the bergschrund.

He waits for Mick — *what's he doing?*

Mick rappels down after him. But hey, what's going on? Why is he doing that? James watches as his friend steps out sideways off the rock, sees him place his feet on the steep snow slope in the gully, then remove his man-made protection from the rock. All that James can think of is that he plans to make an ice bollard for himself.

FASCINATING FACT
A Rock Climber's Technical Jargon

Man-made anchors to tie ropes to can take many forms, for instance: a short piece of rope or webbing may be tied to a rock to form a loop; a tapered piece of aluminum connected to a wire loop may be wedged into a crack so it bears weight; a piton is a thin, wedge-shaped metal blade that is hammered into a thin crack; or an ice bollard may be used. Ice bollards are cheap, but time-consuming, and are built by chiselling a large ring in the ice, or hard snow. A post is left in the centre and the middle of the rope tied around it; the softer the snow, the larger the bollard that is needed. Man-made anchors are reusable, so climbers take care not to leave them behind.

But somehow in the process, Mick falls, and his fall is unprotected. James watches in horror as his body tumbles 70 feet down the mountainside. He watches as he goes into freefall for the last 30 feet to land close to where he himself is standing. James grabs hold of him to prevent him from falling further into the bergschrund. He's stunned at what has just happened and for a moment feels paralyzed. He notices that the sun has risen higher and chased away shadows from the rugged mountain slopes. It's about eleven o'clock in the morning. Here is his friend and long-time climbing partner lying unconscious on a shaky ice platform high in the mountains. No sign of any other life up here. Worst of all, neither of them has a radio or cell phone.

With a plummeting sensation in his heart, James knows it will take six to eight hours for him to hike to the helicopter meeting spot — a meeting not scheduled to take place for 24 hours. He stares over a cold, impersonal universe of snow and granite, and knows that his only option is to stay beside his unconscious friend, to try to keep him warm.

Hey, but there is human life on the mountain after all! James hears rocks falling, and hope rising, looks over to see two figures scaling a slope right next to the peak that he and Mick are on.

Two long-time climbing partners have come to Squamish to tackle the vertical cliffs. Val Fraser hears what she thinks are rocks falling and thinks it must be the noise of heli-logging across the valley. But wait — those sound like human voices. They can't be! She looks across to the base of the snow gully and is astonished to see two people — but only one of them upright. She stares. Suddenly the world goes quiet. Out of the silence she hears one of the climbers begin yelling — shouting that the other is badly injured and can't move. She calls out to her partner, Peder Ourum, and both shout across to the other party: "What can we do? Do you have a cell phone? … We have one … We'll get to you as fast as we can."

Peder takes out his cell phone and calls his wife. "Please get through to the Whistler — you know, the helicopter long-line rescue service (HFRS)," he says urgently. Then he and Val immediately begin a difficult and dangerous climb up toward the ledge where Mick lies. They are not quite at the top, but can see over its lip. They take a look at the white-faced James, at the moaning and near-comatose Mick, then at the small rocky platform.

"Oh my God, it looks like it might give way any moment." Val mutters this under her breath. If any of them are to survive, they'll have to make this rocky ledge secure somehow — and do it fast. And somehow they have to help the fellow lying on the ice to keep warm — and alive! — while they wait for help.

Val and Peder begin building an anchor with an ice axe and ice screw. They tie one rope in. Val fastens herself to the end, and then jumps up and onto the mushroom. It holds, but it's very thin and could break off and plunge her all the way down into the bergschrund. Her blood chills at the thought. But now she's on it, and greeting James and Mick.

Poor Mick. He lies twisted on the snow, a little bloodied, but conscious and answering questions. Val immediately places rope, a backpack, jacket, and fleece-lined shirt under him for padding. The injured man looks up at her, puzzled. Who is this stranger who has magically appeared out of the snowy void? His big hands are wet and cold. Val struggles to get them into James's gloves — "like trying to dress a child," she says.

The rescue platform remains shaky. The three climbers know that the ice anchor has to be backed up to the rock on one side of the bergschrund, and to the glacier on the other, so that none of them fall off. In silence, they build an anchor on the top surface of the mushroom. As soon as they finish, they hear a thump — then another and another. Part of the mushroom gives way and white spray flies up all about them. The whole area on which they are perched could collapse at any moment. They stare anxiously at each other. Then, in silence, each searches for other anchors along the solid rock on one side, and the glacier on the other, so that they can back up their existing anchors.

After this is done they feel a little more secure. They turn their attention to the patient. Mick is conscious and in pain. He complains about the cold, and about his legs. He has a broken nose and his eyes are beginning to swell, but there are no signs of other bruising or bleeding. Val pads him further with ropes and jackets.

There's nothing else she or any of them can do; they'll just have to wait.

Time passes. "I think it's got stuck," Val says fretfully, her voice echoing into the silence of the mountains. "It's not moving — nothing moves. But hey, did you hear that? — It must be the chopper — thank God! Oh, but it doesn't see us — it's flying right past!"

||||||||||||||||

Brad Thompson is at home with his family, along with his friend Nathan Dubeck, when both their pagers go off. It is a summons from the Royal Canadian Mounted Police: *Will all SAR members report immediately to Warehouse Number 5.*

Both men hold the title of deputy co-ordinator and search manager for the town's volunteer Search and Rescue team, directed by the RCMP. They look at each other, both flooded by a sudden rush of adrenaline. A call to a rescue — as opposed to a search — is much more dramatic and urgent.

Brad picks up the phone and calls for details while Nathan searches for a helicopter company that might be available, as they'll need a chopper to carry the Search and Rescue team up into the mountains. Brad's adrenaline pumps as he begins phoning all the SAR members. He asks them to report to number 5 Progress Way, the address for their Search and Rescue headquarters. He tells them it's for immediate action to get a rescue mission prepared for the Tantalus Range of mountains.

> **FASCINATING FACT**
> **In the Mind of a Rescuer**
>
> What goes through the mind of a rescuer when he/she gets a call like this? First, time is critical because, if someone has severe injuries, they can become more life-threatening as time passes. A Search and Rescue worker must immediately put himself into rescue mode, run his mind over all the training he's been through, and imagine how things should unfold in the first ten minutes after the call. It's an awesome responsibility: the rescuer worries about saving lives, but also about the cost — he's held accountable for this, too.

On this same day and time, John Willcox is already up. Sun streams through the east-facing windows of his home in the mountains and he stands admiring the view. The Tantalus Range shines in the distance, tantalizing, as always — one of John's favourite spots around Squamish. He is startled out of his reverie by the screech of his pager. *RCMP dispatch: Injured climber on Tantalus Range.*

A second page comes minutes later: *All available SAR members please attend Number 5 Warehouse for an injured climber.* John's pulse quickens and he feels a rush of adrenaline. He leaves his wife,

> **FASCINATING FACT**
> **Origin of the Name Tantalus**
>
> The Tantalus Range of mountains was named after Tantalus, the Lydian king and son of Zeus, whose name is also at the root of the verb, to tantalize.

FASCINATING FACT
A Third-Level, Advanced Life Support Paramedic

Third tier paramedics are trained for two years in classroom and field. They make advanced diagnoses and perform invasive procedures (airway breathing tubes, intravenous, surgical procedures, and medications administration). The equipment they use is of the sophisticated kind usually found only in a hospital emergency room. Two medics working together can quickly assess patient needs, perform life-saving treatments, talk to an emergency doctor, and package the patient for rapid transport to the most appropriate emergency medical care facility. All the while they provide ongoing care as the patient is being transported to a hospital. If there are multiple patients on the scene, dual medic crews can split up and each takes care of a patient. Enough equipment is available to transport patients in separate vehicles. Transport vehicles can transport multiple patients lying down.

toddler, and new baby, and races to Brackendale where Squamish has its Search and Rescue headquarters. Brad Thompson, acting as co-ordinator, is already there and has placed a call to three helicopter companies. The first to call back will be given the job. Blacktusk Helicopters comes through first, and its staff hired.

"We have a seriously injured climber and time is urgent, so I've asked for a long-line rescue," Brad tells the pilot. "I've got the authority to make this decision," he says, "but I never make it lightly. It involves many highly trained people and a lot of money." He then begins the time-consuming process of organizing the equipment they'll need. Next he has to choose a spot for a heli-pad, and to decide among his group of Search and Rescue workers who he will select to fly to the area. Without question, John Willcox will be one of them. He's a third-level paramedic with advanced training and much experience.

Next, Brad has to decide who will make the rescue plan, who will treat the injured climber, and who will be the person to report all the details to the SAR manager as they become known. Brad leans forward and drops his head in his hands. All the responsibilities and decisions suddenly seem overwhelming. It's half past noon when the helicopter lifts off. The sun is high above the mountains and the air is cool and clear — different from many other September days when winds blow noisily along the canyons. Before long, they are flying up the west side of Mount Dione, 8,000 feet above sea level. The crew is tense and anxious.

High up on the mountainside, the three climbers do everything they can to look after the severely injured Mick. Their anxiety increases as time passes. Tirelessly they work to secure the ice platform that holds them, but still it seems precarious. They are tied to an ice block, but have no idea how long it will stay in place. Suddenly, out of the silence, they hear it — a chopper! It flies right past them, then circles around and returns, searching for a place to land.

> ## FASCINATING FACT
> ### A Hot Unload
>
> In a "hot" unload, the medical team will move in the moment the helicopter's skids touch the ground. The helicopter will keep its engines and rotors turning, only if the urgency for treating the patient outweighs the risks and difficulties of operating the aircraft. All staff operating within the vicinity of the helicopter should have formal, explicit training in hot operations procedures. Staff involved will be provided with hearing protection.

"We're here, at your three o'clock, about one kilometre out," Peder's voice breaks through the chatter on the helicopter's radio. He tells the pilot to approach a small saddle about a quarter of a kilometre away as a spot for a hot unload.

The pilot gets as close as he possibly can without affecting the climbers huddling on the perilous ice shelf. Wind from his spinning blades could knock them off their small ice perch. He puts both skids on the snow and holds power, his blades turning, until the crew deplanes and unloads all its gear.

"I'll circle above you and send information to the Search and Rescue command," the pilot says as John Willcox and the other two rescuers tumble out of the aircraft. Val's heart jumps with pleasure and relief. She smiles at Mick and says, "Hey, a great bunch of guys has just arrived to help you. Soon we'll all be out of here and this will seem like just a bad dream."

As Peder hikes down to help carry the crew's medical equipment and rope rescue packs, the ice platform rumbles and cracks, then a large horseshoe of the snow collapses and falls with a *whumph* into the bergschrund.

They all look around, terrified.

"It's like an earthquake! Like an avalanche," Val exclaims. "The ice mushroom gave way right where I've been sitting for the past hour, and there's Mick lying just inches from its edge!"

SAR Team member Doug Wood climbs an icy slope. Notice the heavy pack he must carry with him.

The men below also hear the *whumph* as pieces of ice break away close to where James is standing, near Mick's feet. They stare at one another and at Val, whose face is white.

"Hey, we're all still tied into the ice anchor I rigged up," she says suddenly. "But look, our perch is now only about ten feet by twelve, and it's getting smaller all the time." She bites her lower lip to control its trembling.

"How on earth are we all going to fit onto it?" someone asks. "How is John going to work on the patient? How is he going to get up here anyway?"

Below, the three rescuers have now climbed up to the ice platform. Dismay alters their expressions as they look around at the precarious ice mushroom where Mick lies and James crouches silently. They watch Val and Peder working frantically to shore it up, trying to build better anchors: three snow pickets on the snow slope, two ice screws, and an axe in the wall above that will support a rope strung across as a Tyrolean. As soon as they finish, they connect themselves to the rope in case more pieces of ice break off and their platform starts to disappear in bits and pieces from under them.

"Get that ice axe anchor backed up to the rock on one side of the bergschrund," a crisp voice says. "Then to the ice glacier on the other side."

John begins scaling up the ten feet to the platform. With two ice axes, a boost, and a knee hold, he's on it. He goes straight to Mick.

"I have to confess that in this environment, and without my partner, I feel I'm not keeping pace," John says. "I'm finding it hard, and very slow."

Mick is conscious but moaning in pain. John has to examine him, but first he has to remove a helmet, get past zippers and multiple layers of Gore-Tex, all of it restricted by a climbing harness that's tethered to a common anchor. He feels pressured to get treatment started, but first he has to make an official report and get a set of baseline vital signs and report them.

A head-to-toe examination shows a restless, pale, 39-year-old man with a broken and bloodied nose. A man who is complaining of chest, back, and pelvic pain.

"I can't feel his pulse, either at wrist or groin, but he must have one," John says. "I mean, he's talking to me. I can feel the artery in his neck — it's racing at a rate of 104."

After two attempts, he finds himself arm-wrestling his patient as he tries to straighten the man's arm to get a blood pressure reading. Mick becomes even more restless and tries to sit up. It's his last rally before he lapses back into unconsciousness. John gives him a trapezius squeeze but gets no response.

"He's stopped breathing!" he mutters. He yanks an airway out of his pack and rapidly puts the bag valve mask together.

FASCINATING FACT
A Trapezius Squeeze

The trapezius is a flat muscle that extends from the back of the neck to the shoulder girdle. To apply the trapezius squeeze, grab approximately one to two inches of this muscle near the base of the neck, between thumb, index, and middle fingers, then squeeze and twist. It is an ominous sign if the patient does not respond to this painful stimulus.

FASCINATING FACT
Surviving Through the Golden Hour

In emergency medicine, the golden hour is the first 60 minutes after a person is severely injured. It is generally believed that a victim's chances of surviving are greatest if they receive specific care in the operating room in the first hour after a severe injury. Recently the validity of the "golden hour" as a specific timeframe has been questioned, although its principle of getting victims urgently treated is universally accepted.

In cases of severe trauma, especially internal bleeding, nothing can replace surgery. Shock may be a complication if the patient is not managed quickly. Victims have to be transported as fast as possible to specialists at hospital trauma centres. Because some injuries can cause a victim to worsen extremely rapidly, the lag time between injury and treatment should be kept to a bare minimum.

While most medical professionals agree that delays in specific care should be prevented, recent research questions whether there is such a thing as a "golden hour," that there is no scientific basis for it, and no magical time for saving critical patients.

But Doctor R. Adams Cowley says, "There is a golden hour between life and death. If you are critically injured you have less than 60 minutes to survive. You might not die right then; it may be three days or two weeks later — but something has happened in your body that is irreparable."

"I saw how easily it went in," Val says. "That's not a good sign."

John can feel a pulse in Mick's neck, but there likely won't be one for long. "Ventilate him. Quick, bag him — please!" John says urgently to Val. "He's bleeding internally. The only good thing is that he's held out through the golden hour."

It's now six minutes after two in the afternoon, three and a half hours after Mick's fall. His veins are flat, but John thinks that with a lucky stab he can get an IV started. He manages to get an 18-gauge needle into a vein and begin a rapid infusion of normal saline from a one-litre bag he carries in his pack. James holds the bag, while Val checks that Mick still has a pulse. One of the rescuers relays radio communication both ways while two others keep inspecting the ice platform — will it hold them? They must be ready to do something if it shows signs of collapsing. And room on it has to be made for one more rescuer and a stretcher.

Mick is getting worse: his pupils are dilated and he'll need to be ventilated while he's being moved. John makes preparations to put a tube down his throat so he can breathe. This is sometimes awkward under the best of conditions, but up here it will be almost impossible, mostly because of the sun that's reflecting off the snow so that John can't see anything past Mick's teeth. Someone throws a jacket over his head and shoulders to block the glare, and now he can use the light from the laryngoscope. After suctioning, then four tries, he finally manages to pass the tube through Mick's vocal cords and into his trachea.

There is little any of the rest of them can do, except wait. Each stares over a vista of jagged peaks, a vast, impersonal, and cold white world.

Suddenly they hear it! Each looks up, relief flooding their faces. Whistler-Blackcomb Helicopter's A Star circles above them. There's hope at last for the man who lies before them on the ice bollard. And relief for themselves that their ordeal — one that will later seem unimaginable — is soon to be over.

The chopper flies above, then radios that it is off to "burn some fuel."

After conducting a reconnaissance of the rescue scene, the Blackcomb pilot searches for the nearest flat spot to reconfigure. He finds one, just a kilometre to the south. Daryl Kincaid and his crew study the winds, weather, weights, elevation, and how close they are to the rock, as they prepare for the long-line rescue.

The group on the ice platform doesn't know that the Whistler SAR team has only very recently got the equipment and training for this difficult and risky type of rescue. Not only that, although their services have been requested four times since, each has resulted in a no-go decision because the conditions have not been suitable. This call has come close to being yet another no-go when one of the crew hears on the radio that the paramedic has begun cardiopulmonary resuscitation (CPR). This is to be their first actual long-line rescue — and a very tricky and difficult one it's going to be.

Photo courtesy of John Willcox.

The mood at the foot of the mountains at the Command Centre is also tense. A jumble of people are running and yelling, trucks are pulling in and out, phones are ringing — the scene might seem chaotic to a passerby, but order actually prevails under the calm direction of Brad Thompson and Nathan Dubeck.

As he works, Nathan's mind flips back to the time he fell off Brohm Ridge in this range of mountains, and to the other time he helped rescue another young fellow who fell off the

SAR Team member Doug Wood scales a rocky mountain face.

same ridge. He thinks that the big challenge to people on mountains is just this: Not to fall off.

Up on the mountain, John keeps checking Mick's neck for a pulse, and finds none. At 2:32 in the afternoon he begins cardiac compressions. He knows that Mick must be bleeding inside his abdomen, and that compressions won't help start a heart without blood, but he has no other options.

"Where's the chopper gone? Why is it taking so long?" The voices on the ice platform are fretful now, even though all of them understand the time it takes to plan and organize a rescue of this kind. Finally, the helicopter pilot's voice comes on the air. "Listen: before we fly in, we need to know: Does the paramedic wish to escort the patient in flight?"

"Yes."

James has taken over chest compressions. John tries to get the patient in a stiff-neck collar and an orange, cocoon-like wrap so he'll be ready to be put in the clamshell stretcher for air-lifting to the helicopter. While he's doing this, James has to temporarily stop cardiac compressions and bagging.

Wait! Something's not right. Mick is about to be moved, he's being pulled tight, but he's not moving. He's still tied in! James frantically unties a bunch of cords from the anchor and the double fisherman's knot to which the patient is attached through his harness. He yells for a knife, but no one can find one. Val reaches over and struggles until she manages to untie the knot.

John is just about ready. He prepares his pack so that it can be slung below him, off his harness, then puts on a jacket for the short flight.

Tension fills the air as Daryl Kincaid from the Whistler SAR team is lowered with amazing precision onto the ice platform right beside them. He's still attached to the chopper, and dangles from a 100-foot line below it. The stretcher is attached horizontally to him at his waist. Immediately he's tied in to a web of safety lines before he unclips himself from the long-line. He listens as he's briefed on the plan to move Mick into the aerial rescue platform, also known as a Bauman bag. All the while he stares uneasily about him. So many people perched on an ice platform that could break away at any moment. They all know this, and limit their movements to the parts of it that are well supported.

Finally, Mick is secured in the Bauman bag stretcher, Daryl on one side and John on the other. John shortens the utility strap that connects the screamer suit harness to the master-point ring of the aerial rescue platform.

"This places me higher, with my knees pivoting at the edge of the clamshell," John explains. "I've never needed to perform CPR during any of my six previous long-line rescues. This is tough." It is the quiet understatement of a self-deprecating man. But by positioning himself in this way, and with a one-foot extension tube between the bag and valve of his bag valve mask, he is able to rock forward to compress with one hand, then flip his other hand over to squeeze the bag to ventilate. In this way, Mick is carried into the waiting helicopter and is flown directly to the Vancouver General Hospital.

||||||||||||||||||

This entire rescue effort has been an emotional roller coaster ride for all the people involved. Their mood fluctuated with the changes in Mick's condition. There was widespread admiration for John Willcox, who had risked his life for another. John denies he was brave. He had simply done the very best he could under the circumstances. The difficulties had been enormous. The rescue had gone well in all its details but the obstacles were huge. Hopes had been high, but in the end, a young man's life had been lost.

"No one can blame the climbers," John says. "The more rescues I get involved in, the more I realize that people who get lost or injured are not careless of foolish. They've been caught up in a series of small errors that end up in one big event. I've made some of them myself."

This rescue has entered into local lore and legend. It was a good rescue with a bad outcome. It was a very challenging one, and a first for the Whistler team — no dry run for them.

The town of Squamish bears a special burden because of its reputation as a rock climber's paradise: volunteers are needed

FASCINATING FACT
Fascinating Facts About Climbers

Some call climbers "rock jocks." Others hold an image of a climber as a wiry, spidery, long-limbed figure, silent and unknown outside the climbing world. Not many look for publicity — most of them just want a hard, clean climb, then to climb and climb again.

Some people scoff at them and write this sport off as a selfish game that is pointless and undignified.

Climbers will tell you that a climb is a complex journey, both an inner and outer one. It has risk — more than the average glory hunter is willing to take.

"It's like, how far can I go? How much should I push?" says climber John Merrett. "Your limits are not what you think. You ask yourself, 'Was I scared?' Yes — I was scared silly."

"You rely only on yourself and your own fortitude," he says. "You look for obstacles rather than avoid them."

Another climber says, "A serious commitment to climbing exacts a terrible price: losing a friend, and another and another. But you can't live without it."

"This sport makes you think about life — about yours, and all others. Of course there's a risk, but it's calculated. If you know how to do the equations, you're all right. There are risks to everything. A rock is a rock, it doesn't change. It's the things you do that make the difference. If you're not able to do a climb, it's because of you, not the rock."

"It's different in other sports, where you have to rely on others. Here it is just you. You have two hours to climb this rock that's 400 feet high. You decide not to put anchors in the rock at intervals of five feet because it takes so much time. Instead, you put them in at ten or more feet, and you take a calculated risk."

who are willing to give a lot of time and effort to maintain their expertise; to train others; and to organize, obtain, and maintain expensive equipment. Demands are made on the town for funds, and then more funds, to enable sophisticated rescue efforts such as this one to happen.

Photo courtesy of John Willcox.

From left to right: climber Peder Ourom, Doug Wood, Hugh Ackroyd, and John Willcox.

4 Jumping into the Abyss

Alberta, 1995

Jim Thoreson was at home, about to serve up a pile of barbecued steaks, when the phone rang. He picked it up. No Mayday call, but the summons for a search; a distress signal coming from an emergency beacon somewhere deep in the Rocky Mountains.

"Need your help," said a voice from the Rescue Centre in Winnipeg (JRCC)."You're closest to where the signal is coming from — would your team do a search?"

Jim, a retired RCMP officer, now an aircraft navigator from Red Deer, is a member of a group called the Civil Air Search and Rescue Association (CASARA). He's well-known for dedicating his time to volunteer aerial search and rescue. Okay! No time to waste: He hustled to prepare his navigational gear and dress himself for the extreme cold. Quickly he wrapped himself in lined boots, long johns, heavy coat, mitts, and scarves. He picked up

FASCINATING FACT
Where Is Revelstoke?

It is located near Mount Revelstoke National Park and Glacier Park, a year-round playground with some of the most spectacular scenery in British Columbia. In the early 1900s it was known as The Mountain Paradise. Now it is proclaimed as the capital of Canada's Alps.

FASCINATING FACT
ELTs and How Emergency Beacons Work

Thirteen years ago, before ELTs came into use, rescuers could have spent weeks or months looking for an airplane that had crashed in the Rocky Mountains.

The ELT system came into being in 1982 when the United States launched two weather satellites with search and rescue abilities (SARSAT). The Russians have two similar Cospass satellites in orbit. The four satellites work together as a team, scanning the Earth for ELT signals. They are in polar orbits that enable them to scan the entire surface of the planet in 1,400-kilometre-wide swathes as it rotates below them.

In Canada, satellite dishes located in Edmonton, Alberta; Churchill, Manitoba; and Goose Bay, Newfoundland monitor the satellites. Alerts are relayed to the Armed Forces Rescue Coordination Centre in Trenton, Ontario.

ETLs are supposed to emit a signal only when jarred into life by a crash. In the event the crash hasn't done the job properly, crash survivors can switch on the ELT manually. A rough landing can also trigger an ELT. The Trenton Rescue Coordination Centre gets two or three false alarms a day, and this is why an initial signal is treated only as an alert, even though a satellite can pinpoint a suspected crash site within five kilometres.

An ELT signal doesn't give the identity of an airplane. That can only be established through reports of overdue planes.

When an ELT signal is picked up by a second satellite and can't be explained as a false alarm, the centre in Trenton swings into action. Supervisors inform the nearest SAR centre, the nearest group of civilian searchers, local police forces, and Transport Canada's area of Control Centres.

Other aircraft can lend a hand. Commercial passenger planes have ELT monitors on board. They are constantly switched on, their pilots listening for a signal on the 121.5 megahertz band. Flying at 9,000 metres above sea level, hundreds of commercial jets are available to help rescuers pinpoint ELT signals.

On the Friday afternoon that Kurt Schultz's plane crashed, a battery-powered electronic device the size of a loaf of bread sent out a cry for help. The signal was picked up by a satellite orbiting 450 kilometres above. It led a privately operated plane to the wreckage within four hours. Several hours after that, two military Search and Rescue Technicians (SAR Techs) parachuted into the site.

the phone to Jerry Mulder, pilot and owner of a Grumman Tiger aircraft who would fly him and two spotters — Ken Brown and Bert Lougheed — to the area. Next he phoned search headquarters to get flight planning: latitude, longitude, and a more accurate location for the distress signal.

Okay, all ready. Bert phoned the Rescue Centre (JRCC) to say the group was prepared to take off, and received new information: A pilot had called the Centre to say that his buddies were to have arrived at Revelstoke, but hadn't shown up.

The flight path of the missing plane happened to be in the same area that the Emergency Locator Transmitter (ELT) was coming from.

"An overdue aircraft on a flight path matching the ELT location — this ramped up the rescue call to the next level," Jim said. "Now we've got not just an ELT signalling — you get many false alarms — but a plane that's gone down. Our sense of urgency was bumped up a notch and we just took off. We heard the

JRCC had scrambled a Hercules aircraft from Winnipeg. It will take it three and a half hours [for it to get there], but only one for us to get close to Revelstoke."

The little plane with four volunteer rescuers took off into the early wintry darkness. No moon in the night sky, just a sprinkling of stars above the jagged mountain peaks where they were headed.

"It was difficult, and I was a little apprehensive," pilot Jerry Mulder said. "We had no visibility — only the darkness of the trees and whiteness of snow — we couldn't even see an outline of the mountains. I had to fly using instruments. The evening was very cold and we flew through snow showers. It was late. We had no clear signal and it would be like looking for a needle in a haystack. I also had to worry about fuel."

As the crew flew through a brief snowstorm they learned of another aircraft already out looking for the downed plane. Two American search and rescue satellites had picked up the ELT signal, but had given a wrong location for the crash site — this was because the signal waves were bouncing off the surrounding mountains.

Jerry continued to gain altitude. He needed to fly high since they were in the mountains, and in the dark. But they had a problem: Above 10,000 feet, crew members are required to use oxygen. Both Jerry and Jim had been trained in high altitude indoctrination since there were no portable oxygen systems at the time. Because of this, they easily recognized the symptoms of hypoxia.

"We talked about what we should do," Jim said. "We'd be flying for an unknown period of time at a height where we should use it. Without it we might develop symptoms, and endanger ourselves. None of us were smokers, and we agreed to monitor each other's movements and actions. As soon as we could, we'd drop to a lower

FASCINATING FACT
What Is Hypoxia?

Hypoxia is a pathological condition in which the whole body is deprived of an adequate oxygen supply. Hypoxia where there is complete deprivation of oxygen supply is called anoxia. Symptoms of hypoxia depend on how severe it is, and how fast it develops. In altitude sickness, hypoxia develops gradually. Symptoms include headaches, shortness of breath, a feeling of euphoria, and nausea. In severe hypoxia, or hypoxia of very rapid onset, changes in levels of consciousness, seizures, coma, or death may occur.

altitude, absorb some oxygen, and go back up again. We know we can stay at high altitudes for only short periods.

"Our small plane flew around for over an hour and a half, searching for a signal — but it jumped all over the place. We heard it clearly at times, but mostly it remained faint. Jerry tried to pinpoint it, to home into it, but the signal kept bouncing. He talked to the crew of other aircraft also looking for it. One pilot gave coordinates where he'd heard the signal, and we set course for that location.

"Other pilots also picked it up: a private plane that was flying at 4,500 metres, and a commercial jet at 9,000 metres. Each heard it only briefly, and neither of them could pinpoint the site. But we knew we must be close. On a hunch, we turned north up a box canyon and stayed above its rim."

"Our direction-finding homer pointed to the left," Jerry said. "We were headed in a westerly direction and could see Highway 93 — the main highway between Banff and Jasper. We saw car headlights on it, and also on Highway 11. Suddenly a light shone out of the darkness and beamed up from the place where the homer was pointing.

"Then we heard it: The faint sounds of a signal. It grew in intensity, only to abruptly disappear and we found ourselves in the electronic cone of silence that exists directly above a transmitter."

Jerry turned his aircraft and headed straight for the spot where he'd first heard it — dense mountain country with no roads anywhere. Then, out of the silence of the night, they heard it again, this time a strong, rapid signal — beep ... beep ... beep. The time was 10:15 p.m. They flew closer and it was then that they glimpsed through the darkness what might be the wreckage of a small plane. They stared at each other in sudden silence. Jerry immediately sent a message to the JRCC to say he thought they had found the missing plane deep in a canyon in the Rockies, right over the spot where the distress signal beeped. He turned his Grumman Tiger and circled overhead twice at 10,000 feet, repeatedly flashing his lights.

Don't lose the signal. Stay where you are. A message came back from the JRCC. *The Hercules aircraft is still an hour and a half away.* And so the little plane hung about the mountains, flashing its lights to give encouragement to victims who might be alive somewhere in the canyon. When the Hercules aircraft eventually came close to the spot where the Grumman Tiger was circling, the pilot said, "We want you to break off, go land in Rocky Mountain House, get some rooms and have a rest. We'll need you for an early morning takeoff. Phone and check in with them when you've landed. We'll stay here and look after everything, and our Search and Rescue Technicians (SAR Techs) will prepare to jump down to the crash site."

"We didn't sleep at all," Jim said. "We kept wondering what was happening out there, and wondering were those people alive?"

||||||||||||||||||||

Report back to the JRCC [Joint Rescue Coordination Centre in Trenton]. *You are needed for a search and rescue mission.*

This message reached young Mark Holoshka one evening in late January. He raced off to 435 Squadron to find out the nature of it — that a distress signal had been picked up somewhere in the mountains southwest of Rocky Mountain House in Alberta.

Quite new to the business of rescue missions — in fact he was a rookie and had not yet had a real-life operation — he wanted one badly. All the practice jumps had been done as well as all his training as a Search and Rescue Technician for the Armed Forces. Now he just waited. Because there were many false alarms he shouldn't get too hyped up, but his head spun.

"You don't know what's going on," he said. "Where this will lead … what you will have to do. Lots of things race through your head. I mean, training is training, but it's not the real world. Nothing prepares you for what's out there. Am I afraid? Only of the unknown because I've not been on a real mission before. Also, there are things you have to do that you know you're not going to be thrilled about. But all your training and discipline will help you learn to suppress your feelings.

"Don Peters is the senior guy and will be our team leader. We got more information as we prepared to fly. When we were told that an aircraft had probably gone down, the adrenaline started pumping and we got busy preparing our equipment: parachutes first. Next we pulled all the equipment from their boxes, and because we didn't yet know exactly what we'd need, we got everything ready."

FASCINATING FACT
What Is TAWS?

TAWS is a system that provides pilots or navigators of an aircraft with a view of the ground and obstacles on it. It helps them to fly safely and avoid anything that could endanger them, for example, cables, a dark night, or bad weather.

If a small plane had crashed in the Rockies, people in it must surely be dead or dying: So thought the two SAR Techs. The pilot of the CASARA plane said he'd received a signal — an SOS — so someone must be alive. The pilot, using a system known as TAWS, circled the Hercules at 12,000 feet above the spot where the signal was coming from.

The crew threw down a TRON radio, and watched. No one picked it up.

Maybe they don't see it, Don thought, not wanting to believe it was because no one was alive. "Not knowing, we threw down survival gear — toboggans full of stuff," he said. "We were going to jump down to get these guys but can only carry so much with us when we drop — that's why we kicked out survival gear in advance. Unfortunately, because of winds that blow in a circular fashion in the valley, most of it flew all over the place."

Ten-man survival kits, and toboggans containing 300 pounds of equipment, were dropped from the Hercules. Most of it scattered about the sides of the valleys. The pilot struggled to keep flying 2,000 feet above the tallest peak, and this meant the toboggans had to be dropped from the same height — 12,000 feet, and into a canyon! Turbulence pushed the aircraft around as the toboggans were dropped and they continued to drift across the valley. The crew found it all very challenging.

Another difficulty was that the aircraft ramp had to stay open while the gear was dropped, and later for the SAR Techs to jump from. This meant the air in the Hercules was not pressurized. The crew should have been wearing oxygen masks while they set up, but since they were kept in the rear of the aircraft, they couldn't get to them. (This problem has since been rectified.)

"We worked for two hours with limited oxygen while we got our stuff ready," Mark said. "It gave me a major migraine headache, but I had to jump with it."

The two SAR Techs were ready. This was to be Mark's first, and a big one. Don looked at him.

"Look, this is risky — you're sure you want to do it?"

"Yeah, I do," Mark said immediately … *I have to get this under my belt.*

If he were asked, he'd agree to dropping into a burning bush with little chance of survival, Don thought.

The jump was not a typical one. It was night. It had to be made from a high altitude into a rocky canyon or small valley — dangerous because the snow-covered ground might be hiding rocks; because winds could be a problem since they were never the same. The jumper could slip when he landed, whack his head, and smack up his body. The temperature was extremely cold. Not least, the jumper couldn't know what he would find at the bottom — a group of people alive but injured — or all of them dead.

A clear Plexiglas door was lowered to act as a platform so that the jumpers could see the ground below. Flares were thrown down. Don, fully kilted with bush suit and helmet on, survival gear in front, stood on the platform, calculating. Time to call a drop: He turned to his partner and said, "Go!"

Mark stepped off. He fell through the air carrying 70 pounds of equipment on his back. Through thin, minus 20 degree air he flew, with a steerable parachute that allowed him to accurately direct his flight path, deep into a canyon. All the while the Hercules crew dropped flares to light up a ghostly scene of mountainous peaks and valleys for him.

As he fell, Mark worried about many things: About the equipment scattered all over the valley — how would they get it? Where was his partner? — He should have been able to see him with light from the flares, or even from reflection on the snow.

I can't find Don, and I'm worried. We're supposed to meet up in the air and I'm to follow him to the ground. I don't know where he is … what's happened to him? … Why can't I see him anywhere?

"I was getting a bit freaked out about these things," he confessed.

FASCINATING FACT
What Is a Steerable Parachute?

This is a parachute of enormous size that can be steered. It pulls off a jumper's back and opens up automatically, which means the jumper does not have to pull any cords. It is similar to those used by the famed Canadian Forces Skyhawks jumping team.

FASCINATING FACT
What Is Being "Hung Up"?

This term means that the SAR Tech is stuck outside the aircraft, hooked to it, and is not able to release his parachute. He has to be breamed back inside the aircraft by a hoisting system. But Don Peters got hung up by his survival pack inside the aircraft.

"It got worse: Suddenly the flares being thrown dropped behind another mountain and I was totally in the dark. I saw nothing, but knew I must be getting close to the ground. Without warning, I landed. Hard! I'd chosen not to release my survival pack ahead of me in case it drifted off like all the other survival gear. I rolled with it. Then I struggled to my feet.

"*Where's Don?* I couldn't see him anywhere so I got on my radio and called up to the Hercules."

"He's been hung up."

"No, don't tell him that!" Don, still in the aircraft, overheard this. He had indeed been hung up. He'd been ready to go, but gear lay scattered everywhere in the Hercules and his survival bag got stuck on the side door near the spotter's chair.

He tried to push it out of the way so he could exit the aircraft, but couldn't do it, and missed his timing. Immediately he stopped and released himself from his survival bag.

"It's like this," he said. "When the last man jumps out, the loadmaster will say *the jumper is away, the chute is clear*. But when I didn't drop, he couldn't say that. I went on the intercom and said *Stop drop! I'm hung up. I'm stuck on my survival bag. Do another circuit, then I'll jump*. The pilot has to come around a second time before I can go."

"I made it clear the second time," Don said. "I was flying down the mountain ridges when I saw it: the wreckage of a plane smashed in half with parts of it strewn everywhere. I thought, holy cow, no one in there could be alive. Five people? So: three dead, one critically injured, and the other alive — that's what I guessed. I mean, one of them had to be, because we'd seen a fire.

"I landed easily and upright, close to Mark. We checked each other out — always the first thing we have to do before we head to the crash site. When he'd jumped I'd seen the risers come up and rip his helmet off. Now I watched him pull a red beret out of his pocket and stick it on his head."

iiiiiiiiiiiiiiiiiiiiii

Kurt Schultz lay twisted in pain on the snow. His back must have broken, and no wonder! The miracle was that any of them were alive, yet here were his mates, chopping pine branches and lighting a fire. One began setting up a primitive camp near the tree line using whatever they had been able to salvage from the plane.

Photo courtesy of John Willcox.

This photo of Paramedic John Willcox extracting a climber from the mountains shows just how difficult it is to transport a heavily laden toboggan or stretcher over Canada's rugged terrain.

His thoughts raced. *Okay, we've landed on snow.* "We didn't stop dead enough to kill us. I'm thinking … thinking … Everything seemed so dead quiet. Just the silence of the mountains, rows of dark pines trees. No other life — well, we wouldn't see it anyway. We were in a canyon, but one that zigzagged all around us with lots of ridges running up the valleys — a sort of U-shaped or box canyon. I looked at my watch — 3:40 in the afternoon."

Okay. What to do first? As passenger Tony Warren would later report, "Pilot Kurt Schultz lay injured amid the wreckage of his downed aircraft in the depths of a box canyon in the Rocky Mountains. The first thing he did was get himself up and go through a checklist of how to signal for help. He told us how to turn on the emergency locator. Then he explained in detail how to operate the radio in the crushed cockpit. But it didn't work, and we didn't know for sure if anybody would ever hear the signal from the emergency beacon."

"I was in my T-shirt," Kurt said. "Better get on my coat and ski boots before I freeze. A couple of the guys were out in the snow picking up the bits and pieces of the plane. The radio? I knew it wouldn't work because it had been separated from the antenna. But it was still on, with the navigational light on the wing still running. I'd turned off the electrics from the cockpit, but now I saw they wouldn't go off and fuel spewed out of the wing. Suddenly I'm scared. But then I saw it dissipating quickly into the snow — not enough heat to blow us up at that point — and too cold to ignite. This was all good; the fuel would just pour into the snow and vaporize.

"We had struggled toward the tree line to set up camp. I'd asked the guys to go back to the plane and get the ELT. We selected the ON button. Then we saw it had actually gone off when we crashed. Great! It will tell somebody where we are, and even if we're all dead, we'll be found.

"I think I had some intense moments, and was in a lot of pain. But all the time I kept thinking we better start taking care of ourselves and our gear. Then another hot pain would shoot right down my back and I'd collapse on the ground. I was lying in agony in the snow, rolling my eyes, when I saw it right beside my head: A beat-up, chewed-up bottle of Tylenol. I took all five that were left in it.

"I don't know how much time passed, but I managed to get up to try to help the guys who were still busy collecting all the stuff they could: a door, a chair, gear from the survival bags, flares, and a magnesium light — the type of flashlight the police carry. We found a little bit of food and walked all this stuff to the tree line about 150 metres up a south-facing ridge. The guys kept chopping up some pine branches to feed the fire.

"Were we going to get rescued? — This question ran around in my mind like an ache. With a flicker of hope I remembered I'd notified my partner of our plans. He would phone Revelstoke to check that we'd arrived. He'd find that we hadn't. Then he would call the JRCC to tell them about our no-show. That would be the start of a rescue. For now we had to stay alive.

"People would soon come looking for us, they'd be out searching. This is what I kept telling myself. Even if we were in a bad place they'd find us. I've been in nasty places before, dropped into some awful canyons as a bush flyer, but never bumped into turbulence like this — pretty interesting stuff! One of our guys sat in the snow flipping through a magazine he'd picked up from the wreckage. 'So, what do you think?' I said. At first we joked around a bit, thinking to put a good spin on it and pass the time. I guessed it would take rescuers a couple of hours to figure out where we were. Another hour to make a decision — then to call somebody — the SAR people would send out the CASARA group to search for us, then launch the Hercules aircraft with Techs on board.

"One of our guys picked up the axe and kept chopping at green pine branches. A good signal fire, we thought. But mostly it gave off a lot of smoke. If you're looking down at it you won't see it — but they might see our flashlight.

"Two to three hours passed and we were sitting about on the snow, trying to keep the fire going, when we caught sight of an aircraft flying over us — my partner's plane! We jumped up and sent up some flares in a direction where we thought they might see us. Sometime later we recognized the Grummar aircraft and knew it to be the CASARA crew. We sent up more flares, saw the Hercules come and make a number of passes, then come down a bit. I knew it was serious work for the pilot because of turbulence at that height.

"We watched them kick packs down to us, probably full of food and water. But because of the turbulence they ended up on three different sides of the canyon, miles apart. The great thing was that they did see our light. They'd remember other crashes in this area and know how bad they were; they'd be thinking we're all dead. Man, they'll be imagining what a nightmare it must be down here, and that one of the SAR Techs will have to jump …"

"My thoughts were interrupted by a yell, and our five pairs of eyes stared as weird shadows danced on the snow. High magnesium flares lit up the whole canyon like the sudden arrival of daytime. Then a figure dropped out of the sky. His parachute was like a big Canadian flag. With him came a splatter of coloured lights that were being dropped by parachute at the same time. Next minute another figure spiralled out of the darkness and dropped down only about ten feet from us. We sat, mesmerized, watching the strange-looking figures as they walked toward each other; watched as they stripped survival bags from their bodies, disconnected their parachutes and folded them up. They checked the other out, and only then walked over to us."

"How many in the plane?" the one called Mark asked without preliminaries.

"We ordered pizza five hours ago — where've you been?" This came from the fellow in the chair.

"You're in a good mood … How many in the plane?" Mark asked again.

"Five."

"You're all here?"

"Yeah."

"And you're all alive — Wow. Great news!"

Another, who had been cutting pine branches, stopped, put down his axe, and sank in the snow.

Don's eyes had been raking in the scene: Three men huddled over a smoking fire, one in a chair, and one sunk in the snow. *They would have struggled to keep the fire alive throughout the night*, he thought. *They don't have shelter. One seems to have a serious back injury, and another has on only a light wind jacket. I've got another jacket underneath — better give him mine.* He removed his parka and slung it around the man. *I'll be okay if I keep moving around — and he has to keep moving too. Someone has to get to the toboggan with all the survival gear in it and bring it back to the group. So it has to be the two of us.*

"I went off," Don said. "I took with me the man I gave my parka to, to get him warmed up a bit."

The toboggan, with gear for the SAR Techs — their food, shelter and equipment, as well as major supplies such as splints and backboards — was stuck on a snowy ridge on the side of a valley. Don looked at the distance between it and the line of trees where the group was huddled, and at the deep snow drifts. He'd achieved endurance training, and he knew his limits. His calculations told him he'd have strength enough to make it there and drag it back to the group. That he and Mark could set up a camp with tents and a stove burning.

"'Let's go,' I said to the survivor

FASCINATING FACT
More About a SAR Tech's Survival Bag

This is like a big rucksack or hiker's bag. It is inserted into a specially made parachute bag that is folded up. It has a strap, a quick-release hook, and another hook that attaches onto the parachutist. It is known as SARPEL — SAR Parachute Equipment-Lowering System. When a jumper drops into a crash situation, he quickly disconnects it and it hangs 15 to 50 feet below him. He can choose to ride with it and take it down with him. He can also choose to release it on the ground before him if he thinks he might have a rocky landing. His choice depends on his situation. It is never lowered when the drop is made through trees because it could get the parachutist hung up.

A SAR Tech will typically release the pack he's carrying before he lands, but Mark felt reluctant to do this because of all the gear they had already lost on the mountain slopes. He didn't want to lose what he was carrying, so chose not to release it, deciding instead to land with it.

to whom I'd given my jacket, and the two of us trudged through snow drifts up to our waists to reach it. I pushed myself to the edge of my limits to reach the toboggan — there were actually two of them strapped together with their bottoms outward. One had split in half. I yanked it from a punch hole in the hard snow. Once I'd got it, I jumped on it and rode it down the hill — great toboggan ride!"

FASCINATING FACT
What Are KED Boards?

KED is an acronym for Kendrick Extraction Device. It is used to immobilize a person with an injury to neck and back so that no further injury occurs while the person is being transported.

"With Don gone up the slopes," Mark said, "I began working with the few medical supplies I'd carried with me when I'd jumped. I checked over the crash victims, set out my equipment in the snow, and began first-aid treatment. Even though the men had started a fire and begun looking after themselves, they were all very, very cold. They seemed to just sit back and relax a bit after we arrived. Suddenly I heard a whooshing of snow and looked up. Don was riding down the slope on the sled. I laughed. Great! I said. Let me get my hands on that.

"I racked it open. First thing I wanted was a KED board for Kurt Schultz. I'd looked him over, and except for lacerations to his face and the pain he was in because of a back injury, he seemed basically okay. I gave him pain-relief medication, then began cutting off his jacket so he could more easily strap him onto the KED board.

"I got the jacket off. *Oh my God, I've missed something!* I was looking down at a blood-soaked T-shirt. The man must have been hemorrhaging from his chest and I'd missed it.

"'Don't worry, it's only blood from my head that's spilled onto my shirt,' Kurt said.

"As soon as I'd finished treating the men, I worked to set up a camp as comfortable as I could make it in the conditions. I hauled in survival gear from the toboggan; inflated the mattresses — very slow when you've got no pumps. In fact, everything slowed down because of the extreme cold. Getting the tent set up was time consuming too, but I got the guys to help me. After Don came back from a second foray up the slopes to get another sled, he looked surprised to see how much the camp had taken shape — 'Good stuff,' he said."

Under the two SAR Techs' hands, a tent with a floor arose on the snowy slope. Sleeping bags were laid out, and extra jackets distributed for everyone. Mark lit up a Coleman stove to give heat, and for cooking a stew.

"Eat it. It's warm and full of protein," Don said. He looked at Mark who sat silently, not touching it. "Come on, you better eat something," he said.

"I'm okay," Mark answered.

"No, you better eat. You don't know when you'll get your next meal."

In silence, the men ate the meal cooked for them on the small stove. It was a surreal experience, an involuntary camping out in one of the Earth's most remote and inhospitable places. At this point they were all reasonably comfortable and prepared to spend the night. The time was close to midnight. Don radioed to the Hercules crew to say that everyone was okay and they could go off — they must surely be almost out of fuel.

The Hercules crew hovered high above the little camp site until five in the morning. Throughout the night they kept dropping flares to help light the area for the SAR Techs.

No shortage of potential rescuers waited for news about the men who had crashed in the mountains. SAR Techs Captain Ben Massicotte and Captain Jay McCallum in Edmonton, together with Flight Engineer Corporal Mark Anderson were among them. Each was told to get some rest on Friday night because they might be headed to a mountain rescue at four-thirty Saturday morning. With a sense of urgency, each departed for the Canadian Armed Forces 408 Squadron in Namao where they immediately swung into action: the powerful twin-engine Huey helicopter must be prepared. At the first streak of light in the sky they

FASCINATING FACT
More Facts About the Huey Helicopter

Hueys are widely used military helicopters, also known as the Bell UH-1 series Iroquois. They began arriving in Vietnam in 1963. Before the end of that war, more than 5,000 of these versatile aircraft were introduced into Southeast Asia.

They are used for medical evacuations, command and control, air assault, transporting personnel and material, and as gunships. They are the most widely used helicopter in the world. More than 9,000 have been produced between the 1950s and the present. The Huey is flown today by pilots in about 40 countries.

would descend into the mountains.

At six in the morning they lifted off, headed southwest to Rocky Mountain House, and into the mountains. The pilot descended into the canyon but stuck to the upwind mountain ridges where wind would least likely affect it. By

> ## FASCINATING FACT
> ### Heli-Skiing Airplanes
>
> These aircraft have snowshoes i.e. plastic on the back of their skids to prevent them from dropping too far into the snow. The skids also help keep the tail rudder up.

eight, the pilot began guiding his aircraft down snowy mountain ridges toward the little camp set up by the two SAR Techs the night they jumped. He landed his craft on snow skids, not more than 75 metres from the tent and the camp at the base of a line of trees.

When all survivors had been bundled into the chopper, the pilot headed for Calgary's Foothills Hospital. En route, the survivors persuaded him to fly to Edmonton where they all lived.

Three walked off the helicopter without help. Two suffered serious injuries and had to be carried off on stretchers, directly into the University of Alberta Hospital. Only Kurt Schultz was required to remain overnight.

The Huey's two experienced military helicopter pilots afterwards commented that they found it hard to believe that these people had walked away from such a shocking plane crash.

"We thought they'd be in much worse shape than they were," Captain Ben Massicotte said, and his partner Jay McCallum echoed how surprising it was that they could walk away mostly unscathed from a small crushed airplane that had pancaked on a snowy mountain ridge in a canyon, and then split in half.

"It happened like this," pilot Kurt Schultz explained from his hospital bed. "It popped into my head one day to get in some good skiing, so I called up some of my mates and said, how about spending

> ## FASCINATING FACT
> ### Rules for Flying
>
> Pilots are required to file a flight itinerary. This means they must let someone know where they plan to arrive, and when. If they don't show up, that person must phone JRCC and tell them that the plane has not arrived.

a couple of days at Revelstoke? I have a twin-engine Cessna 337 that can take a few of us. The guys were all for it and we decided on a date and time. I got busy and filed a flight notification with some fellows I'd partnered up with who own another airplane — the rules are that you have to tell somebody of your plans.

"Everything was organized. I stowed all the bags, survival kits, suitcases, boots, skis, jackets — all the stuff we'd need — in a cargo pod in the bottom of the plane. Because it was warm inside, I took off my jacket and wore just my T-shirt. I was all ready to go and waiting for the others. They didn't show up. I waited two hours before they arrived.

"It was late. Too late to go — but I checked the weather anyway. Not so great, and lower than I would have liked. I knew there was no lighting at Revelstoke and that it's a tricky airport to get into. I thought about these things, but I said, *okay, let's just go.*

"So the five of us took off. On this early morning in January, we flew out from Edmonton for a skiing holiday. We headed for Revelstoke, near Glacier National Park in the Rockies, all of us anticipating a couple of days of hard, back-country skiing.

"Only 45 minutes into the flight, the trouble began. We're climbing, cruising at 8,500 feet. Suddenly we get caught in a big mass of air that's going down — like an elevator that you're in and you can't do anything but go down with it. We come around the corner of the mountain and hit a real punch of turbulence. I'm scared. I've been flying for a few years but never came across something like this — it's weird. It's like somebody grabbed the tale of the plane and gave it a good shake. Then everything seemed normal.

"I'm thinking we must have hit mountain wave turbulence. I make a turn to come back around, and that's when we get nailed by it. We're up on our side, literally at 90 degrees, with the wings perpendicular to the

FASCINATING FACT
Do You Know What a Mountain Wave Is? — A Pilot's Account

"It is extreme turbulence and downdraft where air comes up a valley — in this case, the Great Divide. It builds in power as it rushes up a canyon. In this particular area just east of the Great Divide, air runs down the canyon, hits a ridgeline, comes back up, then goes down again on the other side. When it hits something, it speeds up — as when you're driving and the air accelerates. On the other side, the air is really motoring, so you end up in a parcel of air that is descending." — *Kurt Schultz.*

horizon. We're heading down, but I regain a bit of control. I need to go left and get us righted before we hit the ground. I push my foot hard to the floor and it's like, ughh ... Next thing we're kind of rolling, descending into a bit of a ball, and then flying out of it. I'm doing everything in my power to get us to go left but can barely control the plane.

"Now we're in a cruise, a little more than 1,000 feet below where we'd just been. But there is no flying out of it. I mean the plane doesn't have the guts to fly out of something like this. We're dropping like a rock, pretty much out of control ... so ... this is it! Suddenly, we hit an outcrop. We bump up a bit, get a little bit airborne and bounce again. The nose comes up. We hit a piece of rock. Bounce over a ravine and hit another chunk of rock on the other side. The engine stops. The plane starts to come apart. Everything shuts down.

"This was it: We were all going to die, I was sure of it. All the time I'd tried hard to keep control of the plane, but didn't think it would do anything ... I knew we were dead, 100 percent sure we were all going to die. It went through my head that my mother was going to be pissed at me. She'd be mad. I heard her voice again in my head: *Jeez, Kurt, should you be jumping off that cliff?* Hers was the voice of reason. My dad? Well, he'd say, *Ah, go for it, son.* But my mum — she won't be happy.

"The plane cracks and shudders and we're sliding ... sliding ... we go about 150 metres through deep snow. We'd been going up an incline at about 140 miles an hour and we smacked into a mountain. From 8,500 feet we hit the ground at 7,200 feet — dropped 1,000 feet in ten seconds and gone 100 metres through the air!

"Everything went quiet, and our plane ended up sideways. It had split right in half just behind the second row of seats — the roof, the tail, and the wings all torn off. But I was alive! I looked down at the ground. It was all weird. I turned around and thought I saw the guy in the third row back looking up at the sky. Next thing, I couldn't see him and thought he'd gone far into the quick somewhere. For a moment I thought about myself and fingered my face. A bit of the Plexiglas window had cut it up. I looked over at Craig who was sitting beside me not making any noise. He'd got a bit of the fuselage right on the noggin, and it knocked him cold; he was bleeding from the head ... I was bleeding ... I turned around again but couldn't see the guys in the row behind me. I yelled something, and suddenly their heads popped up — they'd been trying to stay alive by keeping them tight to their knees. They were in shock. One had a bit of a laceration to the head, but said he was fine.

"Wow, what the heck happened? Oh man. Where was the guy in the back row? I thought the rear of the plane that snapped off had departed off the side of the cliff somewhere.

"He said, 'I'm here. I'm okay, but please stop bleeding on me.'"

"What?"

"I looked, and saw one of the guys in the second row dripping blood on him. I turned again to look at Craig beside me. He was out cold. Oh man! This was urgent. I fumbled frantically with my harness, jumped from the plane, and walked around the front. I got Craig out of his harness and pulled him out. He was unconscious and I tried to wake him up. I'm thinking *this is not good; this is not a good thing.* Just as I was pulling him up against the side of the plane, he came to — a big relief. That's when I suddenly felt a horrible twitch in my back and fell to the ground. All the time the adrenaline had been pumping and it must have stopped me from feeling anything. *I think I've broken my back … my Mum's going to have something to say!*"

So did the National Transportation Safety Board have something to say? They insisted on interviewing pilot Kurt Schultz even as he lay in his hospital bed.

"They wanted me to assume all the blame," he said. "And I deserved some because I made mistakes. The weather wasn't great. I felt pushed by time because everybody was late and I said, *oh, let's just go,* so our plans changed by two hours. Also, there is no lighting at Revelstoke and it's a tricky airport. I thought that by admitting my mistakes, other people could learn from them. The Safety Board wanted to fix blame on my flying. They insisted I'd stalled my plane. 'You tried to out-climb the mountains and stalled,' they said."

"Ask any of us, I said. We didn't try to out-climb any situation. If I'd tried to, I wouldn't have bounced off a rock, split apart, and gone sliding up a ridge."

SAR Tech Mark Holoshka had some comments to make after his first "for-real" jump. "It was challenging going in there," he said. "Quite hard to get into — and especially since we had to operate at high altitudes. We also had trouble getting survival stuff into the narrow canyon where the men were. What we dropped scattered everywhere. I mean, the main medical kit fell on a ridge high above the crash site. But Don did manage to get to it.

"It was my first for-real jump since I began training in 1993. Lucky it was a textbook night rescue. Conditions for a jump were good: A clear night with no wind. But the location of the crash site was inside a fairly large box canyon with many large ridges running off it — this was difficult.

"I landed within ten feet of the men standing around a camp fire on a bluff above the wrecked plane. The victims helped themselves in their own rescue and did a good job of it with little experience or real formal training. They performed a lot of the key basic things that helped them survive for the first few hours after their crash. We took them home, but they certainly got themselves off to a good start. We were all air-lifted at once, except for Don who stayed behind to pick up all the gear."

ıııııııııııııııı

Why did Mark want to do this jump in spite of the hazards? Why does he choose to do this kind of work? Mark has been asked such questions, and he answers, "You rise to the challenge. You've put yourself in the position to do this kind of this work, so you better rise to it."

Honour was bestowed on the two SAR Techs, Don Peters and Mark Holoshka, when each was awarded the Meritorious Service Medal. This award, instituted in 1984, recognizes a military deed of activity performed in an outstanding, professional manner according to a high standard that brings considerable benefit or honour to the Canadian Forces.

A second award was also bestowed on the volunteer group of rescuers who first found the crash victims. On behalf of the CASARA crew — Jim Thoreson, Bert Lougheed, and Ken Brown — pilot Jerry Mulder was awarded the Mynarski Trophy from the National Search and Rescue Secretariat, the highest award given for excellence in field and air Search and Rescue.

The four men are volunteer members of the Civil Air Search and Rescue, an association founded in 1986. Its 3,300 volunteers in Alberta alone spend 10,000 hours a year honing their skills and speeding to help people in trouble.

As vice president of CASARA and a retired Mountie, Jim Thoreson told me how he got into this potentially dangerous and often difficult work.

"We've all got one cause in mind — to work for the lost person," he said. "It's a kinship. It started because there was no aviation for rescues in Alberta, no organized search effort except for the military at the time, no private aircraft. No one knew what to do, or how to do searches. The Alberta Aviation Council, with the help of the provincial government, set up a program to study the situation, and then an organization was created to search for missing people and downed aircraft. I got my licence in 1976. I dreamed of having my pilot's licence — I tell you there was a need! My philosophy was that if I got into trouble, I'd hope someone would come looking for me. I wanted to do the best I could for someone else."

CASARA is now the only aerial search organization in Alberta since the departure of 435 Rescue Squadron from CFB Edmonton in 1994.

SAR Tech Don Peters now lives in Australia, Mark Holoshka on Vancouver Island, and Kurt Schultz in New Zealand — does Kurt miss his mother's voice saying, *Jeez, Kurt, should you be …?*

5 A Burning Boat

Kingston, Ontario, 1853
Conception Bay, Newfoundland, 2007

"The Thousand Islands ... a melancholy bode," wrote the governor of New France in the year 1650. "... nothing agreeable about them other than their multitude ... a bunch of little islands where even the experienced pilot will sometimes lose himself...."

Four centuries ago, the St. Lawrence River was so hard to navigate that the French planted a type of poplar tree all along a channel that followed the north shore of Lake Ontario. They believed this would prevent them from getting lost. It would show them how to get back the way they had come — not so different from Hansel and Gretel and the trail of bread crumbs in the woods.

At the time, people who lived on the shores around Brockville would sit and watch ships passing; see them get lost in endless channels among the islands. Occasionally they witnessed terrible shipwrecks — many of them caused by fire on board the vessel. They could tell immediately if it was fire, by the flames that lit up the sky. Those were the days when sailors feared fire more than water.

In April 1853, the passenger steamer *Ocean Wave* called into the port of Kingston. The schooner had been built in Montreal to trade between New York and Hamilton, Ontario. Passengers were boarded, and cordwood stacked high on deck. Then freight was added: 3,000 barrels of flour, hundreds of bags of seed grain, 300 kegs of butter, 60 barrels of potash, large numbers of hams, and other materials.

Next, workers piled fat fuel under the steamer's boilers. Then came more logs full of flammable sap that were also piled on the deck. All this would give plenty of heat to keep up steam pressure for the engines. The ship was now ready to leave. Because she was so fully loaded, her passage would be slow.

The *Ocean Wave* sailed before midnight. By one o'clock in the morning she was 23 miles from Kingston and two miles off Duck Islands.

Just after 1:30 a.m., a sailor came running to tell the purser of a fire on board. Already flames were leaping up from the boiler room. The heat was intense. Flames, fanned by northwest winds, spread so fast the crew had no time to get to their lifeboats.

Together with the passengers they rushed to get water buckets that hung on the cabin walls, but the walls had already been burned almost to the floor. In just 23 minutes, the ship had become a flaming furnace that lit up the sky for many miles around. People living on nearby Duck Islands said they could read by light from the burning ship.

Two passing schooners called the *Emblem* and the *Georgina* could see the terrible plight of the *Ocean Wave* by the brilliant light in the sky. Their captains thrust their engines full steam and headed toward it. Sailors on these steam ships repeatedly risked their lives making daring runs to the burning ship to try and get the people off. In the end, 21 people survived, and 28 died. All the flour, the grain, hams, butter, and potash perished — a big blow to the local economy, and to the maritime interests of the time.

Today, a Coast Guard search and rescue coxswain and his crew patrol the area around the Duck and the Thousand Islands. If they know the history of this area, they'll feel grateful that the work they do is in this century and not those before. Back then, a wreck was not usually discovered until morning, perhaps many hours after a ship had been struck. And many wrecks occurred there because charting was poor; ships got lost in fog and in all the many channels that flowed among the islands. When storms threatened, they ran for shelter in artificial harbours. Often they missed and hit sandbanks, rocky shores, and piers. Sudden gales blew up that swept crew fore and aft and into the rigging. There they clung until they perished — or were rescued — against all odds.

When a shipwreck was found, a courier on horseback might be directed to the local station — if there was one — and a telegram sent. A train might be taken to the site of the shipwreck. Horses were hitched to draw a boat wagon with is crew down to the shore, close to where the ship had foundered. There they would launch their small boat into the huge inland seas, their men straining at the oars. Seas often overwhelmed the little boat and capsized it. The crew clung to it while it shuddered over rocks and, with luck, grounded itself on shore.

FASCINATING FACT
Who Is Given Ultimate Responsibility for Search and Rescue?

In 1947, the Royal Canadian Air Force (RCAF) was given a mandate to coordinate air resources to go to the aid of people in trouble. In 1951, an added responsibility was to coordinate all Search and Rescue operations in Canada.

The Military's particular component of Canada's Search and Rescue teams is comprised of 650 people. This includes air crew — pilots, air navigators, flight engineers, and loadmasters (in charge of gear) — and Search and Rescue Technicians. In addition, there are ground crew and air controllers.

Today, sailors no longer fear fire on board because it has become rare. Boats are generally constructed of fibreglass or steel, and the days of steamships whose engines have to be fed with wood are long gone. In the twenty-first century, a sailor — or anyone in distress in Canada — has all the resources of the Canadian Coast Guard and the Armed Forces to call upon. These organizations also have contracts with other government and commercial organizations that will provide any necessary assistance, depending on what is needed.

While rare, fire might still break out at sea, as young Michael Petten knows. As the crew of the fishing boat *Nautical Legacy* knows.

In May 2007, Michael Petten is 18 years old, and the youngest of six sailors who have been at sea for the past five days. It's been a busy time dragging shrimp and lifting crab from pots. The boat is fully loaded with its catch and is headed for home. This has been Michael's first fishing trip. He's just finished his hour's watch and is ready for bed. Fisherman Carl Avery is to relieve him.

FASCINATING FACT
Measuring in Knots and What Navigators Used for Speed Measurement Before the GPS?

In earlier centuries, the only way to measure a ship's speed was for the sailors to throw a wooden panel overboard into the sea and watch the rope that was attached to it unwinding from the reel. The faster the ship was moving forward, the faster the rope would unwind. By tying knots in the rope every 50 feet and then counting how many knots went overboard in 30 seconds (measured on a sand glass at that time) the sailors could judge the speed that the ship was travelling. This is how the nautical speed unit came into existence and why it is called a *knot*.

One knot equals one nautical mile per hour.

This is how the math works out: the number of knots going overboard in 30 seconds is exactly the number of nautical miles per hour at which the ship is cruising. If 10 knots go overboard in half a minute, then the ship is moving forward at a speed of 10 knots or 10 nautical miles per hour— about 11.5 standard miles (18.2 kilometres) per hour.

1 nautical mile = 1.15 miles = 1.82 kilometres = 6,067 feet

The term *nautical mile* remains in use to this day.

Global Positioning System

GPS, or the Global Positioning System, is used for navigating, and for determining exactly where your location is — that is, exactly where on Earth you are, wherever you are!

It was originally developed by the U.S. Department of Defense in 1973 to help soldiers — in military vehicles, aircraft, ships, or on the ground — to know their exact position anywhere in the world.

Today, GPS has been adopted widely for use in both the commercial and the scientific worlds. Commercially, the system is used for positioning and navigating in cars, aircraft, watercraft, and for all types of outdoor recreational activities including hiking, rock climbing, fishing, and canoeing.

In the scientific world, GPS is used by meteorologists for weather forecasting and for global climate studies. Geologists also make use of it because it is a highly accurate method of surveying the surface as well as the interior makeup of our planet. In earthquake studies it is used to measure the movement of tectonic plates during, as well as in between, earthquakes.

A ship's speed can be determined by using GPS. The system works through a network of 24 Earth satellites that send radio signals back to the surface. Each signal contains exact position and time— measured by an on-board atomic clock — and travels at the speed of light.

"The wind is up pretty strong," Michael says. "I'm off to my bunk for a sleep."

Michael is tired, and just wants to get back home. He's learned that the fishing life is not an easy one, but what else will he do? He hunkers down in his bunk bed and falls at once into a deep sleep.

The other five sailors too are tired. The *Nautical Legacy* is 153 kilometres from the Cape St. Francis shore in Conception Bay, and it will take 12 hours to get in. The good thing is that the weather seems to be clearing and the fog lifting. Winds are still blowing hard, but dropping. *Nautical Legacy* is making good time in spite of seas that swell up to two metres high. No danger from anywhere; they can all relax.

Michael is in deep slumber. Carl stands near the wheelhouse, his turn on watch. This has been a good fishing trip but he, too, is glad to be heading home. He stares over a choppy sea. Suddenly he thinks he can smell something funny, like something's burning. It must be that someone left the toaster on — or the frying on — something like that. He wrinkles his brow and sniffs again — definitely smoke. Something's burning. He goes to the galley to check, opens the door, and intense heat rushes out to meet him. A fire with leaping flames races along the floor toward him. He claps a hand over his eyes and shouts as he runs back up to the wheelhouse.

"Fire on the decks. *Fire!*" he yells.

In a small room a few steps from the wheelhouse, the captain is asleep in his bunk. Carl bursts in on him and cries, "We got fire on board! *Fire!*"

Harold Stokes, the skipper, jumps up to check on it. He opens the door to the engine room. Thick smoke and a burst of hot air hit him. He slams the engine room door shut and yells to Carl, "Get the boys up and the suits. Be ready to abandon ship!" Flames lick along the floor and curl up at him, but he's oblivious to shooting pain from burns to his face. He's also not aware that flames have burned part of his suit. He dashes back to the wheelhouse.

"Get the men up," he yells again. "Get ready to abandon ship!"

It doesn't take long. The five men sleep in two rooms with a partition between them. One has three bunk beds and the other has two. Carl yells at the sleeping fishermen and they wake up, rubbing sleep from their eyes. They pull on jackets and trousers and come running. One man races to the locker behind the galley and grabs a bunch of survival suits and carries them to the top deck.

Michael, only half an hour into his sleep, lies blissfully unaware of the commotion. But somewhere in his sleep-drugged brain the word *fire* zings. He too rubs his eyes, then jumps up.

FASCINATING FACT
What Are ELT and EPIRB?

ELT stands for emergency locator transmitter. EPIRB means emergency position-indicating radio beacon. The origins of the two terms are different: ELT signals aeronautical distress and an EPIRB signals maritime. They are often used interchangeably.

Each sends out a signal, a cry for help, and the signal is picked up by a satellite orbiting 450 kilometres above the Earth.

FASCINATING FACT
Mayday

Mayday is an emergency code word used internationally as a distress signal in radio communications. It is derived from the French *venez m'aider* meaning "come to my aid" or "come to help me." It is used to signal a life-threatening emergency by many groups that include: police forces, pilots, the fire brigade, and transportation organizations. The call is always given three times in a row, *Mayday Mayday Mayday*, to prevent anyone mistaking it for some similar-sounding phrase under noisy conditions or to distinguish an actual Mayday call from a message *about* a Mayday call.

A Mayday situation is one in which a vessel, aircraft, vehicle, or person is in extreme danger and needs urgent help. Examples of grave and imminent danger in which a Mayday call would be appropriate: fire, explosion, or sinking. It can only be made when life or craft is in imminent danger of death or destruction.

Mayday calls can be made on any frequency, and when a call is made, no other radio traffic is allowed except to help in the emergency. Although Mayday calls will be understood regardless of the radio frequency on which it is broadcast, first-line response organizations such as the Coast Guard and Air Traffic Control monitor designated channels: marine MF on 2182 marine VHF Channel 16 (156.8 MHz); and air band frequencies of 121.5 MHz and 243.0 MHz

A Mayday call is roughly equivalent to a Morse code SOS, or a telephone call to the emergency services.

He rolls from his bunk and, wearing nothing but shorts and a T-shirt, stumbles from the room and into the galley. But already his way is blocked by curling tongues of flame that lick along the floor straight at him. He stares, horrified and momentarily paralyzed. *He has to get to the locker room. He must grab his survival suit.* But a wall of smoke curls about him. His throat starts to swell and he coughs. His eyes water. Frantically he turns around, only to find his path blocked in the other direction. He's hemmed in on all sides by smoke and leaping flames. He's trapped. Then another realization dawns on him — *he's alone* — alone on a ship on fire. Panic rises.

"Don't panic, don't panic," he mutters. "That way I'm dead all the faster." Slowly, deliberately, he returns to his bunkroom, only to find that it's already filling with smoke. Calmly he looks about him. Where, and how to escape? Ha! The emergency hatch, the small skylight in the ceiling … maybe … maybe … He climbs up and yanks at it.

On top of the wheelhouse, Harold is into his neon orange survival suit and struggles to portside to get to the EPIRB.

He must get to it, to manually release it, but he sees with dismay that his way is blocked by suffocating smoke that wraps itself over the entire port side. He can't get to it! Flames are already leaping toward the bow. Then, with heart sinking, he watches the EPIRB burning, then plummeting over the side of the boat. No signal will go out. Immediately he turns to the radio and declares a Mayday.

The Nautical Legacy *burns out of control.*

Courtesy of the Department of Fisheries and Oceans.

The time is 12:22 p.m. He needs to know if the Mayday has been received, and prays for a quick response. No response comes.

The men huddle on the top deck in front of the wheelhouse, the only part of the boat that gives protection from the leaping flames and from thick, choking smoke.

It dawns on them suddenly that Michael is not with them, and it's then they hear a noise coming from a bunkroom hatch. It's the young lad, locked in by fire and smoke, the skylight his only escape. Two men run to help him wrench open the hatch and pull him through it.

"The life raft," someone yells. "Get the raft!" But the lifeboat is anchored near the rear of the burning boat and is already half consumed by flames. Now there is nothing to save them.

"Get your survival suits on," orders the skipper to those not yet into them. A pile of yellow suits lie on deck. Harold watches his men pull them on. Thank God he went through the exercise of making each one practise getting into them before they left on this fishing trip. But wait — there are six men, and only five survival suits. There is a horrified silence.

Harold is shocked. The sailor, who grabbed what he thought were all the suits, looks from one man to another, stunned. He turns his eyes to Michael who stands a few feet from him, shivering in his underclothes.

"I couldn't get to the locker to grab mine because of the fire," Michael says simply.

Five men are in their bright yellow survival suits and one in just his underwear, all huddling in front of the wheelhouse. The heavy silence continues, broken by men shouting as tongues of flame race furiously from the stern toward the bow; flames that crackle along the deck and leap up to blacken the windows. Harold knows that any moment now they'll blow out, and the ship will explode.

The sailors turn their eyes to Michael. He stands gripping the railing, staring down at the cruel North Atlantic. Its dark waters heave closer and closer to what remains of the deck of the little fishing boat. Its water temperature is just two degrees. Harold, as skipper, can't tell Michael — can't tell any of them — that help will come because he can't be sure his Mayday has been received.

The flames leap closer. A window cracks, then blows out, but still the sailors put off jumping into a black sea that's creeping up all around them. They *must* jump. It might save their lives. In their suits they can survive for an hour — maybe longer. But no one wants to be the first because of the lad in his underwear.

"We don't want to jump," crewman Owen Power says, "because we know that the longer Michael is in the water, the chances of him surviving isn't good. He won't be living long in that freezing water. He's standing there in nothing but his shirt and shorts and he's got no protection."

They look at each other, then at the captain. *I'll give the kid my suit*, thinks Harold, and begins to remove it, but another thought occurs to him — that it won't even fit him.

Flames crackle closer and another window explodes. The ship has now burned almost to the water line.

"We gotta jump," the skipper says with urgency. "The windows will all be blown out any minute." Still no one moves.

Michael stares into the icy sea, then back at the burning ship. This is his terrible dilemma:

to burn, or freeze to death. He knows his mates have delayed jumping because of him, but they're taking chances with their lives. Abruptly he makes the decision for them. He picks up a rope on a buoy and ties one end of it to his waist — not to keep himself afloat, but to make the recovery of his body easier if he dies. But Michael will not have his young life extinguished without a fight. If he ties the buoy close to his body he might save himself getting internal injuries from the 20-foot jump into the water.

For a few seconds longer he stares at a roiling sea. *When I jump, it'll take the air right outta me lungs,* he thinks. *Like a sledgehammer it'll hit me.*

He jumps. With heavy hearts, the remaining fishermen follow him into the frigid ocean. Harold has taken rope with him, and once they are all in the water he orders them to stay close to each other. He then ties them all together. In case of rescue — or even of death — none of them will drift off and be lost.

The heads of six fishermen bob about in swells that crash over them and buffet them. No one speaks and time passes, time that seems endless and surely must have stopped. An hour passes and the sailors begin to lose hope as the cold seeps through their suits. Ricky has suffered smoke inhalation and his suit is leaking. Each man huddles about Michael, as though the closeness of their bodies will warm him. Two have their legs wrapped around him. They know he can't possibly last much longer.

Michael, attached to the buoy, endures being swamped by the ocean swells that he can't ride out like his survival-suited buddies. Miserably he feels the effects of being in the water: he's cold, so cold! His mind doesn't seem to be working properly. He's beginning not to care so much. He feels sleepy. This tells him his body temperature is getting dangerously low. He loses consciousness. When it returns briefly here and there, he figures he's only got about another 10 or 15 minutes to live.

"I keep asking Michael, I say to him, 'How you getting on,'" Harold says, "but the boy doesn't answer."

Harold is not to know — none of the fishermen can know — that back on shore their families have learned of the fire and begun a prayer chain for them, a chain that soon spreads to other communities.

A boat on fire! The emergency Mayday call has been received after all, although Captain Stokes is not to know it. His urgent message is heard at the Rescue Squadron headquarters in Gander, Newfoundland, and the Joint Rescue Coordination Centre (JRCC) in Nova Scotia. Officers in Gander immediately call the Department of Fisheries and Oceans (DFO) to ask for the use of an aircraft — that it is needed for an emergency rescue.

DFO in turn asks for the services of a provincial King Air Surveillance aircraft. Its job is to fly to the burning boat to try to find the men in the water. Simultaneously the JRCC sends a Hercules aircraft from Greenwood, Nova Scotia, and a Squadron 103 Search and Rescue helicopter from Gander. And this is not all: The Canadian Coast Guard sends two of its ships, and three Coast Guard Auxiliary vessels, all to the site of the burning boat.

At noon on a heavily overcast day in Gander, the crew from the Squadron 103 search and rescue helicopter have just returned from lunch.

"As a standby crew we always eat together," Search and Rescue Technician (SAR Tech) Dave Payne says. "We'd just got into the hangar when the call came through that a boat was on fire and men in it were getting ready to abandon ship. We immediately swung into action."

Pilot Captain Christopher Hertin immediately checks that he has sufficient fuel for the distance. Co-pilot Captain Wayne Timbury checks the weather: Heavy low cloud, and foggy.

"Okay to travel," he says. "Get the chopper fuelled up, as much as she can carry."

The pilot orders the crew to remove equipment that won't be needed and to check for everything they do need: a rescue stretcher called a stokes litter; a rescue basket of the rigid kind that can be hooked onto a winch; rescue strops or horse collars that are strapped around a victim's body; personal diving and other equipment.

"You just never know what you're getting into," Dave Payne says. "So you prepare everything. We've got our dry suits with us … we're ready … the pilot says, *let's go*! And we lift off."

Just 22 minutes pass from the time the crew receives the call to the time they are airborne.

"But almost as soon as we're up in the air we run into bad weather," Captain Timbury says. "When we left Gander it wasn't horrible, but as we fly, visibility gets worse and we have to go up above the cloud cover."

Inside the chopper the two SAR Techs are busy getting organized.

"Brad Power is our second SAR Tech," Dave says. "He's just gotten into this. It's his first big mission and a good one to start his career off with. The two of us get into our dry suits, get out sleeping bags for survivors, put any equipment we

FASCINATING FACT
About Breaking Rules of Speed

Flight regulations tell a pilot how fast he's allowed to go, but he can break those rules in emergency situations. Speed restrictions are imposed for mechanical reasons. To go beyond them is not so much breaking rules, as it is taking a calculated risk with the aircraft when it seems necessary to save lives.

won't need out of the way … There are six people in the water, so we prepare seats, beds, and stretchers for them all. Then we plan what we'll do. We talk through the different scenarios we could face, like, are the men in the water, or are they in a life raft? What condition are they in? — There are different ways of handling things. All we know is that these men are abandoning ship."

"We're flying above the clouds," Captain Timbury says. "We're speeding faster than the rules allow. We're 20 miles from the fishing boat, but there's some weather out there — thick cloud, high winds and rain. We have to break through to get there as fast as we possibly can."

The first to get to the burning boat is the King Air fixed-wing aircraft. As it arrives over the spot in the ocean identified by the Mayday call, the heavy clouds break apart. Sun shines out from a suddenly clear blue sky. The pilot hovers in the area identified on the Mayday. He makes a pass, and second one, and still doesn't spot anything below.

The desperate fishermen see an aircraft flying toward them, watch as it makes several passes back and forth, and zigzags above them. They wave their arms frantically and yell, although they know their voices cannot possibly be heard.

"Hey, kid, the planes are here," one says to Michael, and at the words, there is slight movement in the boy's near-dead body.

"But where's the raft?" another frets. "They haven't dropped us a raft. They don't see us!"

It's only on the third pass over that the pilot sees something in the water — not a ship, which has now burned to the water line some distance away — but a red balloon. The crew then catches sight of heads bobbing in the ocean swells. The pilot needs to get close, but not too close; he needs to be just above the water without hitting it, and without coming too close to the men in it — a tricky bit of manoeuvring. He immediately radios to tell the fishermen they've been spotted and help is on the way. A short ten minutes later, Captain Hertin in the Squadron 103 Search and Rescue helicopter is circling above.

Michael rouses himself at the commotion all about him. He realizes search and rescue people have arrived and asks, "Can I go first?"

For the helicopter crew, an urgent decision must be made about their immediate actions. No time to waste. The gear is all ready … the fellow down there without a survival suit must be brought up at once.

"The Fisheries patrol aircraft was already there," Dave says. "Their cameras have allowed the crew to see six people in the water, and that one of them is not wearing a survival suit. When they tell us this, we know what we need to do first."

Dave knows, as team leader with the most experience, he will be the one to make the jump. Brad will give the fishermen medical attention once they are up in the aircraft.

Dave stands in the doorway of the chopper and stares down at a heaving sea. It's a drop of 30 feet. There are risks to jumping from this height, but he's trained for it. He knows the pilot can't come closer to the water for his own safety, and he must also protect the fishermen from the helicopter's downdraft. For the same reason, Dave deliberately aims to enter the water about 80 feet distant from the men. He makes a side door or free entry, feet pointed, into the seven-foot waves below.

With a rope attached to him that is connected to a rescue basket, he swims with mask, fins and snorkel toward the fishermen. They are tied to one another by a rope, and all have flotation devices attached to their survival suits — "will make my job a lot easier," he says.

"Take him up first," comes a chorus of voices and Michael is

FASCINATING FACT
What Is a Side Door Entry?

A side door entry into the water from a helicopter means to jump into the water as opposed to being hoisted into it.

pointed out to him by several fishermen. Dave swims to the motionless body and finds two others with their legs wrapped around him as though to keep him warm. He cuts the rope that Michael has tied to himself and attached to the fishing buoy.

"Come on, kid, climb on my back and I'll get you into this basket thing," the SAR Tech says. "I have him climb onto my back to keep him above water while I get the basket to him. It means that I'm under water for a while!"

Michael moves. He sees the basket that is to carry him up out of the water, carry him to safety, and tries to grasp it. It takes him two tries before he manages to get himself into it, Dave half pushing him in. "I'm amazed at how coherent he is," Dave says. "How he can obey my commands."

Next thing, Michael is on his way up to the helicopter. He's at its open doorway, but has no strength left. He can't summon up enough to crawl out of the basket. The helicopter crew pulls him out and into the craft. Once inside the helicopter he collapses and drops back into unconsciousness, his legs paralyzed from the cold. Brad Power immediately struggles to get him out of his clothes, wraps him in warmed blankets, and places hot packs around him. He bundles him into a sleeping bag. The crew returns to the job of bringing up the rest of the men.

Down in the water, Dave approaches Harold and helps him into the rescue basket. Ricky Mercer is lying unconscious in the water. His survival suit has leaked and flooded with water. His body temperature has been lowered to the point where he shows symptoms of hypothermia. Complicating this is damage from smoke inhalation. Brad looks him over once he has been hoisted into the helicopter, and immediately administers oxygen — this guy might not survive. He struggles to remove Ricky's wet clothes, gets him into a sleeping bag, and surrounds him with heating pads.

One by one the fishermen are disconnected from the rope that ties them together, Dave swimming each one away from the remaining men, both to protect them from the propeller blast, and the danger of the rescue basket hitting them. He helps each one into it. They are lifted up to the chopper where Brad immediately takes care of them. The whole effort has taken just 18 minutes since the call for help came. Flight engineer and hoist operator Brad Lawrence finally sends the basket down to Dave and brings him up. He closes the aircraft, raises the heat, and the pilot climbs high above the clouds to speed toward St. John's.

"The weather out there is loaded," the captain says. "Low cloud, very foggy, high winds; the cloud is lower than the land and I can't see anything. I have to make a landing using my instruments — something you need to have a lot of practice for, and a lot of skills. We have lots of missions — like this one — where we have to get to people fast because they are in danger of dying; they're near dead."

As the search and rescue helicopter makes its way into St. John's Airport, the rescue team scratches their heads at the way Michael has improved since he was air-lifted up. By the time they reach the tarmac he's ready to walk in his sleeping bag to the waiting ambulance. But after the warming in the helicopter, Michael's internal body temperature is still only at 32 degrees and it will take some time before it climbs back up to the normal 37.

"Given Michael's size, he should have gone into cardiac arrest from the shock of the cold water," the treating doctor says. "In my line of work, I don't impress easily, but this lad really impresses me."

Michael's only after-effects include some tingling in his feet, which should gradually fade with time.

"It's a miracle. He's a miracle," Michael's mother insists, and credits the on-shore prayer chain for saving the life, not just of her son, but of all the sailors on the *Nautical Legacy*.

Doctors check out the other five men in the emergency room at St. John's general hospital. All are doing well, but two need treatment for smoke inhalation, and Ricky for hypothermia. Harold Stokes is treated for burns to his face, burns he didn't know he'd suffered. At some point he had lifted a hand to his stinging face and pulled away some skin, but supposed that it was salt he was rubbing off his face.

Captain Wayne Timbury talks about the danger he faces, that all SAR people sometimes face. He talks about the calculated risks. How he can override flying regulations regarding speed if life is in danger. He also has to justify breaking these rules.

"It takes a long time to achieve the position of pilot, and with it comes lots of responsibility," he says. "Like when you decide you must stand outside the rule book — in other words, break the rules. There are lots of instant decisions and judgments you have to make. Sometimes you have hairy adventures, like sea states 80 feet high. Imagine a SAR Tech having to land on a boat in sea swells that high and you're 450 miles from land.

"Danger comes from water," he continues. "Coming through it, under it, over it, and down to it. And staying above it. You have to judge how much fuel you'll need. You need to watch the winds because they change all the time. You watch for snow. It's a hugely challenging job, and you need all your skills, especially when you have to land in a small village — or in any small space."

Wayne speaks as chief pilot of the Rescue Squadron in Gander, on standby from 8:00 a.m. until 4:00 p.m. He is in charge of pilot training, gives exams, and is responsible for the careers of others, in fact, for their entire welfare.

"Search and Rescue workers — technicians and rescue specialists with the Coast Guard, and pilots and divers — come to this work in different ways," he adds, and talks about his own path to this work.

"I went from university to work in forestry," he said. "Then I worked as a glass blower. I got married, and I needed a job with a decent income, so I became an air cadet, then an officer in pilot training.

"The big thing is to be the best you can in school," he says. "It will make a difference. You will have more choices and you can do many more things. The job I do is a good one: you can go overseas, go anywhere in the world. There are all kinds of opportunities in it."

SAR Tech Dave Payne explains how he got into the Military and spent 13 years in the Air Force. "It took two years for me to get my application accepted for SAR Tech work because it's highly competitive," he says. "I've had a great career in the Air Force: first I was an electronics technician; then I went from fixing planes, to jumping out of them.

Why did he switch to search and rescue work?

"I was always interested in medical things, and helicopters, in parachuting, hoisting, scuba diving, mountain climbing — it's all very appealing. I like physical challenges because they make me feel very alive … there is quite a feeling when you do these things: there's drama, camaraderie … you look after each other, you trust each other with your very life."

He pauses, and then adds that he does feel fear, but he trusts himself to do what it is he has to do.

"Fear of failure is always there," he says, "the fear of doing something not quite right. You rarely fear for your own safety because you're trained, you know what to do and you've done it before … This mission: you don't want to get there with six people alive and not have six alive when you leave. That would really haunt you long afterwards.

"These fishermen did everything right to save their own lives," he adds.

A Coast Guard official also praises Captain Harold Stokes and gives him credit for saving the lives of his crew.

"He stayed to call for help when he could have been putting on his survival suit," the spokesperson says.

"The EPIRB burned with the boat," Captain Christopher Fitzgerald says. "Without the captain making the Mayday call, the *Nautical Legacy* would never have been found."

Harold himself says that the experience hasn't bothered him, although it enters his mind sometimes. "You have to get beyond it," he says. He too credits a prayer chain for their survival, and particularly the miraculous recovery of Michael. It was a chain that rapidly extended from the original small group of friends and family to many of those who heard about it.

Following the successful rescue of six fishermen from their burning boat, Prime Minister Stephen Harper made a weekend visit to Port de Grave, Newfoundland's historic fishing port, to pay homage to the captain and crew of the *Nautical Legacy*. He told them they were proof that the days of the iron men were not yet over.

"People who come from somewhere else sometimes romanticize life in fishing communities," he said. "They don't appreciate how hard this work is, and how dangerous it can be."

He praised the crew for their dedication to safety, and to their training.

"Although what's left of the *Nautical Legacy* is now on the ocean floor," he said, "her legacy is a reminder that emergency training and search and rescue programs are there to keep seafaring Newfoundlanders safe. Survival at sea is a shared responsibility; when rescuers and the rescued know their jobs and do them properly, everyone comes home safe. All of those involved in this harrowing incident applied their training exceptionally well, and it helped save their lives."

"Newfoundlanders are people of the sea," Federal MP Fabian Manning said. "We grow up breathing salt air into our lungs every day. We are proud of who and what we are. Our attachment to the sea has brought many tragedies, but the story of the *Nautical Legacy* is one of survival."

Michael Petten's mother, Sherry, has her own interpretation of this survival story. "It was a Perfect Miracle," she said. "When the author

Coast Guard ships display their firefighting skills.

Courtesy of DFO and the Canadian Coast Guard.

of *The Perfect Storm* wanted to write the book, he had to do a lot of research on why the circumstances or surrounding events caused this to be the perfect storm. All the prevailing winds had to converge in just the exact time and at the exact position that the *Andrea Gail* was. If the wind was a slight degree off course, there would have been no *Perfect Storm*.

"I think when God decided to send us a perfect miracle, He had to do a lot of figuring: about Michael over the years; the choices he made. The fact that Harold, the captain, had all the crew try on their survival suits. The prayer chains …"

Note: No cause for the fire on the *Nautical Legacy*, a fibreglass boat, has ever been found.

6 A New Recruit

Kingston, Ontario

We will go out to save anything that's living and breathing — there's no limit …

"It's only my third day on the job with the Canadian Coast Guard," says Wade Buell. "I'm to be deckhand on the Coast Guard ship, the *Griffin*. I know nothing. I have no clue what to do. The ship is in refit in Thunder Bay so I'm being sent for a couple of shifts to the lifeboat station in Kingston."

The young Buell sleeps his first night uneasily on a hard narrow bed in makeshift accommodation. At two in the morning, the radio phone rings its summons into the trailer, startling him so that he almost falls out of bed. A voice speaks into the silence: "There's a lifejacket floating upriver. Nobody in it. No body, nothing else around — need you to go check it out." The three Coast Guard rescue workers are out of bed, into their clothes, and running from the trailer in what seems to Buell like mere seconds.

Before his eyes are half open he's aboard the Coast Guard vessel, a Boston Whaler that speeds at 50 kilometres an hour upriver. The powerful beam of a searchlight restores riverbanks that disappeared as the night unfolded. A helicopter flies overhead. In the murky darkness of the dead hours, the new recruit clutches tightly to the sides of the boat. The wind whistles, and the choppy waters of the river wash right over.

"I felt a huge rush of adrenaline," says Buell. "The wind, the speed of the boat, the helicopter flying overhead; we're here on the river looking to save someone's life. I think of the poor person half dead in the water, and I say to myself: *This is the kind of thing I want to do for the rest of my life*. I'm like a newborn duckling being imprinted by its mother to a particular kind of a job and a whole way of life." Buell falls silent a moment as he stares out the window over the grey seas of Lake Ontario.

What about the lifejacket?

"We picked it up," he says. "But we never found a boat, a body alive or dead, or anything else.

"In the end, my very first experience with the Coast Guard was nothing more than picking up a lifejacket out of the river. And my first real rescue operation was saving the life, not of a man, a woman, or a child, but of a prize-winning goat from the Welland Canal." Buell laughs as he recalls the goat story — "a real sheepish experience," he says.

Rescue of a Prize Goat
Welland Canal, Ontario

The Welland Canal is a modern-day marvel of engineering; it began with a man and his dream — shipping channels through the canal, to the head of the Great Lakes, through Montreal, and out to the mighty Atlantic. The dream became a reality when the sliver of water that became the first Welland Canal opened in 1829. Along this channel sailed and steamed the world's great ships of commerce, and pleasure boats of all kinds. They traversed the St. Lawrence River to the Great Lakes and into the heart of North America. Guarding their passage were, and are, Coast Guard search and rescue workers whose responsibility it is to help vessels pass through and to rescue anyone in distress.

Today, on a beautifully landscaped arm of land that juts into the waters of Lake Ontario

Courtesy of the National Film Board, Toronto Reference Library Archives.

An aerial view of the spectacular Welland Canal system.

sits the rescue workers' home, a low-slung grey wooden building near the site of an old lighthouse. The station as it is now did not exist when Wade Buell was a young man. In 1978, at the time of his second rescue mission, he slept beside the waters of the canal in a rough trailer, together with two strangers from Port Weller in southern Ontario. Three days into his job, the call had come.

"A goat drowning in the canal up at the locks," says the radio operator. "Owners want to know if you can help get it out."

Buell laughs. "People call us for the most unimaginable things," he says. "They know we'll do everything in the world whatever the situation. There's no limit to what we'll do: The Coast Guard will rescue anything that's living and breathing. We do it because that's the nature of our job. And because we want to."

"A goat! My God, they want us to rescue a goat!" says one of the crew. The summons draws the rescue workers out of bed once again in the early hours of the morning. In a few short minutes, Reg Clark, Bob Whiteside, and the new recruit are on the Coast Guard cutter speeding up river to the lock system on the canal. The lights on the seaway cast yellow beams across the water and on the stream of cars lined up to cross the bridge, stuck there because it is raised for a ship to pass through. Owners are out of their vehicles and hanging over the lock's railings.

A truck was carrying a load of prize-winning goats, the bleating load jammed among cars waiting for the bridge to open. Something had startled the animals and three leapt right off the truck. The driver, a stocky fellow in bright red shirt, shouted as he chased after them. People loitering about the canal joined in. Car horns blared and people laughed — they laughed until someone cried, "There's a goat in the water. A goat's fallen into the lock!"

The truck owners manage to capture two of the runaway goats, but the little one, cornered, panics, climbs up the railings, and leaps into the lock itself, thirty feet below. The crowds scream and point as it frantically swims about the canal.

"It's like a circus when we arrive," says Buell. "We beam our searchlight over the docks, the locks, the ships, the cars, and all the people — amazing how many are up at this time of the night!

"We pilot our boat into the lock. With the beam of our searchlight we catch sight of the little fellow thrashing about in the canal. All we can see is his little head sticking out of the water. He swims to our port side, then goes under it. That makes us worry: he won't have strength to last much longer because he's been in the water a long time. Next thing, he appears over the starboard side of the bow. Unfortunately we can't lean over the sides to try to grab him because there's too much free board. The people above are shouting and laughing and we feel a bit embarrassed. But we really do want to save the little goat."

One of the crew takes a mooring line, makes a lasso, and throws it over the goat's head. Miraculously, the little fellow swims straight into it. The crew tightens it, and on the count of three, gives it a quick hoist. The little goat flies out of the water and lands right in the middle of their deck. It's been done with such skill and speed that the lasso hasn't strangled the little creature. The crowds roar their approval.

"I'm standing by the rail on the starboard side," Buell says. "The goat lands — he looks half drowned, a skinny little thing with his hair plastered to its sides. He scrambles to his feet and gets ready to butt anyone or anything in front of him. I'm within his line of vision, and in range of him. He goes straight for me. He butts me in the side of the leg and afterwards I suffer the worst charley horse I've ever had in my life. I can hardly walk for a week."

To the cheers and the shouts of the crowds, the Coast Guard crew tie the goat to the deck, rev up the boat's engines, and cruise home to their base. They tie the goat to a tree near the trailer to keep him safe until the owners come to claim him — owners who are grateful. In a gruff voice the fellow in the red shirt says, "Thanks again … he's an expensive little beast …"

"A prize-winning goat," says another. "Costly little fellow. Our whole truckload is prize winners, but this one — he's the best of them all."

"A weird affair altogether," says Buell. "We got laughed at by other rescue workers for a long time after."

A Cow That Fell over a Cliff
Burin, Newfoundland

"Have I ever said no to a rescue job, stood it down?" asks Darryl Taylor of the Burin lifeboat station on the southwest coast of Newfoundland. "I tell you, I couldn't turn me back on a person, even if I'm having to ask myself: *Can I get in and get out again, safe?* We don't say no to a person. But there was a time I said no to a cow; three years ago it was, and I said no to a cow that fell over a cliff."

It happened in Port aux Bras, a village where every person knows every other; knows where they are and what they do. And they believe they know what the Coast Guard rescue workers should do. Today, a villager comes to the lifeboat station to ask the crew to go out in the rough seas to rescue his cow that fell over a cliff.

In Port aux Bras, the few cows and sheep kept during spring and summer are grazed on fields around the houses and on land that wanders to the edge of jagged cliffs. Some people tether them; others ask a young person to keep an eye on them to make sure they don't wander. These animals are slaughtered in the fall to provide the winter's meat supply.

On this particular day a cow called Susie has fallen over the cliff. She has landed 60 feet below on rocks that jut above the shoreline. Miraculously she is still alive. Her owners are anxious to retrieve her but, not being able to do it themselves, or knowing how, they ask the Coast Guard crew to go and get her, and bring her to shore in their cutter.

Crew members fire up their fast-rescue, inflatable Zodiac boat. It roars the short distance around the bays to Port aux Bras. Villagers crowd to the top of the cliff, anxious and upset at Susie's piteous mooing. The Search and Rescue workers study the scene and think about what it will take to rescue the animal — and at what risk to themselves. Rocks, sharp as shrapnel, jut out at the foot of the sheer cliffs. Seas rise above them in fury. Winds fling spray high into the air. A cow weighing more than 300 pounds is stuck on rocks that are perilous to approach in these conditions. Alive, she won't fit into their Zodiac. Anyway, they can't drag her on board the cutter in the heavy swells — even if she would fit! The hazards to them in their small boat are huge.

"Sorry, we can't take no risks for a cow," the crew answers. "We'll come back tomorrow if the conditions improve."

In the evening, a man from the village walks the sloping road to the lifeboat station. His purpose is to complain to the Coast Guard crew, to argue about why they will not rescue the cow.

'It's your job," he says. "Don't you care that some in the village are crying because their cow fell over the cliff?"

"I have to explain myself," says Darryl Taylor. "I tell him that absolutely I will risk myself and my crew to go to the cliffs for a child or an adult but not for an animal. For people, I'll stay out all night. I'll do anything." He pauses, then adds, "Will they be crying when the fellow that owns her has her slaughtered for his winter supply of meat? When it comes her time he'll kill her and stick her head on the gate post. She died just a little bit earlier, that's all. If it was a youngster now, I would have stayed out all night.

"Sometimes you have to bite your tongue and say nothing. You have to turn your back and walk away."

The cow, miraculously, is still alive. People throw hay over the edge of the cliff to feed her. Some of it lands close enough for her to munch on. The crew at the station explains to the cow's owner how he might try to retrieve her.

"Wait awhile until the seas are calm," they say. "Take out a flat-bottomed boat. Tow a dory behind it. Go in, tie up her legs, and see if you can haul her into the boat."

This is what the owners do. The sea swells are gentler the day they go out. They tie Susie's legs together, a rope around her massive neck, and heave her into their boat. Crowds yell encouragement from the cliffs above as Susie struggles. The owners sweat and curse as they haul her bulk aboard their nearly-submerged boat.

Susie is fed until the fall, and then slaughtered, as is the custom.

7 A Child Is the World

Fredericton, New Brunswick

"It's like this: Every day you have people you love around you is the best. Every time I see a child, I feel, gosh, he's okay ... he's safe."
—L. Merritt, Rescue Worker

Susie Stockton sits in front of the television, deep into a soap opera. The room feels warm, so she gets up to close the blinds against an afternoon sun that streams in the windows. From time to time she glances through the slats to make sure her four-year-old son Ritchie is still there on his bike. He's dawdling in slow circles about the driveway and talking to his kitten.

Lost in his own little world as usual; his mother smiles as she watches him. He's a good kid, always happy. How he loves to spend time on his bike, and as for that kitten of his — he's crazy about her. Susie turns and glances through the open door into the next room. Her own mother, Gwen, is sitting at the kitchen table playing solitaire.

An hour or more passes before Susie looks out the window again. The time now is between four and five o'clock. The child's bike is in the driveway, but the child is not. And there's no sign of the kitten.

The silence of the forest that crouches closely around the house seems suddenly menacing. The only sounds Susie can hear are a frog croaking and the roar of trucks on the distant highway. Somehow they emphasize the hush. Susie runs outside and calls. She calls over and over.

"Ritchie … Ritchie … Where are you? Come back inside … Ritchie, *where are you?*" She runs to the back of the house to the edge of the woods. It seems to her then that the trees in the great hardwood forest are mocking her. They lean close, as though trying to touch the walls of her house.

No reply comes to the increasingly frantic mother and grandmother. Gwen, not old, but stooped, walks up and down the gravel driveway that leads to the street and to the subdivision proper, all the while calling to her grandson. Susie phones her neighbour, then all her friends and relatives, asking them to come and help search for her boy. The late-summer sun slips slowly toward its horizon and night will soon be encroaching. Susie picks up the phone and dials 911.

The Stockton house is one of two homes that sit at the dead end of a lonely road about one kilometre from a secondary highway. Each house looks as though it's been carved out of the forest and become part of the lush green world of hardwood trees, and of boggy marshland that overlies rock and shale. It's a place where reeds and willows dangle over frog ponds, swamp, and pools of stagnant water. The trees — spruce, pine, and maple — are reflected in the water. Groves of alder are so dense that they make the forest seem like a jungle. Bird and insect life flit about like the boy himself who has to be creeping about inside that forest — where else would he be?

Maybe he's exploring the hollow places in tree trunks where all the little people live, thinks Susie. Like trolls and elves and pixies. Maybe he's fallen asleep under a tree … maybe he's dreaming about lurking black bears, coyotes, or foxes. With this thought, Susie starts to cry.

Corporal Terry Higginson is in a meeting with the local search and rescue group when his pager goes off. He grabs it from his gun belt — part of his Royal Canadian Mounted Police uniform — and listens.

"Child in Beaver Dam missing since five this afternoon …" He leans toward Stephen Moore and whispers, "I might be needing the search team. I'll let you know." Then he's gone.

The 30 members attending a monthly gathering of the York-Sunbury Search and Rescue (SAR) Team have a hard time keeping the meeting going on this warm summer night. They have heard the words whispered — *child missing* — and wonder if they'll be asked to do a search.

Corporal Higginson calls the Communication Centre to get more information as he drives home to pick up his gear. He'll also need his search dog, Dar. He then continues driving toward the Beaver Dam subdivision that lies about 18 kilometres outside Fredericton.

"They call me first because I'm a Mountie, and because I belong to the local search and rescue team," he says. "Also, I'm a search-dog handler. As I learn a few details about this missing boy I begin to think I'll need the team — lucky thing all its members are together tonight. When I get calls like this I know I'll need my dog. I like to take him with me and go on my own to the site first. I have to know if there is a track for this person; I have to get all the important information. Only then will I know for sure if I'll need the SAR team. I also want to see how many people are there already. I need to talk to the mother and find out all I can about the boy. By now it's also getting late in the day — between seven and eight in the evening."

Terry arrives at the Stockton home, astonished at the number of people already milling about. He's disappointed; they have contaminated the area for his dog. It will be much harder now for him to follow the boy's scent. He learns that many people have already gone off into the woods, both on foot and on all-terrain vehicles. He looks about him. Where's the mother? — he needs to talk to her. Susie and Gwen are wandering around on the driveway looking frightened and helpless. Gwen drags fiercely on her cigarette while short, plump Susie runs her hands through her thick chestnut hair as she repeats, "He's only four … he's so little …"

In response to Terry's questions, she answers, "He's about three feet high. He's got thick, chestnut hair, like mine. Brown eyes … I saw him out here in the driveway on his bike … he doesn't wander off — not usually …"

She remembers that Ritchie had been chasing his kitten all afternoon and guesses this is the reason he's gone into the woods — the kitten has run off into them. His bike stands in the driveway, close to the house, but there's no sign of the kitten. Susie starts crying again. When she stops, a vacant look enters her eyes — the look of a person deep in thought, or like someone desperately trying to remember what's just happened, Terry thinks.

Susie is asking herself: *Where was she? What she had she been doing? — Watching television ... oh, why hadn't she been watching him more closely!*

She straightens suddenly and looks Terry in the eye. "My boy is afraid of the dark," she volunteers. "He's afraid of the woods. He doesn't like being alone in there. I know his fears and it really hurts me that he might be lost in there ..."

Terry listens. He makes his decision and picks up his mobile phone and calls the SAR team.

Stephen answers at once. "Okay," he says. "We'll get organized and get ourselves there, fast as we can."

While he waits for the team, Terry walks around the house with Dar. The search dog's nose is to the ground and he's running from one spot to another. Terry follows him behind the house and through patches of nearby woods. Like old friends, he and Dar search together through abandoned vehicles that have been junked on the uncultivated land behind the house. Terry picks through all of the small junk piles. He gives up trying for a track because there are too many people out in the woods. "RCMP search dogs will track only to the freshest scent," he explains.

Terry's call to the SAR team has reached them while their meeting is still in progress. It ends abruptly as they all jump up and make plans to meet, and then race home to get their search gear: A flashlight, warm clothes, compass, GPS, maps, boots, hard hats, rain suits, food, and water — all that's needed to last them for 12 hours — these are the rules.

They all meet. Their convoy of cars turns off the highway at Lord Road, then heads toward a subdivision that spreads itself across both sides of the road. It is a housing area with a sprinkling of businesses, surrounded by a dense mix of hard and softwood forest. They turn onto the lonely gravel road that leads to the two houses at the end.

"It normally takes a couple of hours to prepare for a search, but we got ready in just under one." Stephen picks up the cube van that they use as a command post, and the first thing he does is set up a centre of communications. Then he looks over all the equipment stored in the van.

The team has parked their vehicles in the driveway. Immediately they switch on the generator to light up the entire area. Next they set up a tent. Propane heaters are fired up. At ten in the evening, everything is set up and 35 searchers are organized.

FASCINATING FACT
SAR Team Equipment

All equipment for SAR rescues is stored in a trailer that is attached to the truck. It contains everything the team might need: tents, a generator, portable radio, compasses, redi-packs, a string X box (a measuring device), flagging tape, and first-aid kits.

"First, what we have to understand is the family and, of course, the little boy," Stephen says. "We have to learn what his habits are. You often hear different stories — like this kid's mother told us her child doesn't mind going through the woods. That he'd been there with an uncle the week before. When he does go into it, he usually sticks to the trails and he doesn't wander off. Next thing she tells us he's afraid of the woods. We ask what he looks like, about his health, what he's wearing (a blue T-shirt with a teddy bear imprint on it; brown shorts). We want to know what he carries with him — like candy, because we can look for candy wrappers. We look for anything that will give us a clue.

"Does he have experience in the woods? Is the bike missing? — No. When and where exactly did the mother last see him? When did she notice him missing?"

Corporal Higginson searches the house a second time. Then he heads back outside to search. He takes the boy's uncle with him, two SAR people, and his dog. Together they comb some of the trails. As they walk, they call out to the boy. Soon they are skirting bog and marshy ground, trampling through thick forest undergrowth.

Back at the command post the SAR team is busy planning the technical details of the operation. The question of where to search first is based on what they think has happened. What are the statistical likelihoods of this area over that one? What knowledge do they have of the child? What are their gut feelings? They break up the entire area into manageable segments. Each area is given a grade based on the probability of finding the boy there. SAR members know the statistics: that it's unlikely a child this young will wander further than about 500 metres from his home. They cordon off sections of the wooded area all about, using datum lines.

Each team is given responsibility to search their portion of the forest. One is marked off, then another and another. It is then assigned to well-rehearsed search teams. Other members are organized to work the trails deeper into the forest. Some are sent beyond this on all-terrain vehicles.

Soon the Department of Natural Resources arrives with updated maps of the area. With them they bring more ATVs so they can help search beyond the immediate spots where the child is thought most likely to be. In due course, the Red Cross will also come.

The woods pose a number of dangers to a small boy on his own, including black bears and perhaps a coyote or two. But the greatest danger lies in the nature of the place itself.

"The woods are extremely dense, thick with undergrowth of the kind you have to fight your way through — very unforgiving," Terry says. "You can get tangled up in it, especially at night. You can get snared by dead undergrowth. As well, New Brunswick is very rocky and beneath a thin layer of soil lays shale, sharp and cutting. You could twist your ankle, cut your hands, your feet ..."

How far can a small boy walk in eight hours? A kilometre — maybe a little more. It's possible, but not likely, that he might have crossed over from the confined area. He could have walked across a railway line or a road. The searchers fan themselves out over the areas they've been given to search. Some comb through abandoned cars; some through small buildings attached to houses. Others check out old sheds. Abandoned wells behind the houses are examined — Terry has already scouted about and discovered them.

"Need to check them all," he says to Stephen, and immediately a group scatters and checks on one, then another and another. All are found to be poorly covered with loose boards that could easily be removed. Still no sign of the child ... and no kitten.

The summer night is upon them, the temperature steady at about 15 degrees. Some SAR members walk

FASCINATING FACT
Datum Lines

Datum lines are used to divide up each segment of ground to be searched. It makes the whole area easier to search. A compass is used to run the line to make sure it's straight, and a string X box is used to lay out a visible line — a piece of string — from point A to point B.

the forest on foot to cover the narrow paths. Trails are made by four-wheelers crisscrossing the forest. Each group takes a string box that contains string, like a fishing line, that shows them how far they've travelled. They mark the way with flagging tape so they will know where they've been, and where they will emerge — echoes of Hansel and Gretel and their trail of bread crumbs.

A local woman comes up to Stephen at the command post to say she'd seen the boy near the frog pond that lies right off the road leading into the subdivision — "three o'clock it was when I saw him," she says. As always, this highlights the difficulty a searcher faces: the mother saying her son would not leave the trails, and a neighbour saying she spotted him near the frog pond.

"I mean, it's easy for the kid to walk to the frog pond," the neighbour says. "I know I saw him there." Her insistence changes the focus of the search. Groups go back again to examine the wells. Others stride off to the frog pond, while several search the trails around the home again.

The boy had left his bike behind. His kitten is missing. Did he go chasing his cat?

"Well, he's been known to follow it around," says Susie. "Tinker — she's a new kitten … He loves her … I guess she went missing and he chased after her."

The blackness of a near-rural night, lit up only by the lights powered by the SAR team's generator, envelopes them all. Seventy-five people have been out for hours searching for the child. Among them are professional volunteer searchers, local people, employees of the Department of Natural Resources, and members of the RCMP and the local volunteer fire department. After the neighbour claims she'd seen the child near the frog pond, firemen work for the remainder of the night to drain it in case the child has fallen in. The body of water measures 40 by 60 feet.

"The local people are in danger themselves," says Stephen. "First, they don't know what they're looking for; unknowingly they can remove evidence. When they get here, we register them. We see that they are dressed properly and make sure they know what they are looking for. When the Red Cross gets here, they look after them, but the rules are that the Red Cross doesn't come to a search site until more than 12 hours have passed. Also, we can't get any more help without the agreement of the RCMP — that's why volunteer SAR has to be self-sufficient for up to 12 hours."

FASCINATING FACT
Fascinating Facts About Search Dogs

The RCMP routinely searches the globe for working dogs. Dar was obtained in the former Czechoslovakia in 1996.

"It is not unusual to go so far afield," Corporal Terry Higginson says. "There is a worldwide shortage of good working dogs and it costs a lot to raise them. They are carefully selected for courage and for versatility. Our dogs can search for missing persons, track, get involved in criminal apprehension, and search crime scenes. Some, like Dar, are able to detect explosives and do narcotics work — this is different from the many that can do only one thing.

Terry has always prized the work he does with Dar, who, at the time of this incident, was an eight-year-old male German shepherd, purchased and owned by the RCMP. Dar has always lived with Terry and his family. The corporal says, "I've trained two previous working dogs for the RCMP, and I can honestly say that Dar had been by far the best of the three, the closest canine partner I've had the honour of working with. Our bond runs very deep and would be impossible to break. Right now I'm training a new police service dog because Dar has developed some medical problems and I know his time as a police dog is coming to an end. Long ago, my wife, two boys and I decided that when this happens, we will keep Dar with us as a pet until the end of his time. He's a great dog in every way: dedicated, well balanced, very sociable, and a really great working partner — the best you can get.

"I've been working with dogs since 1993. It puts me on 24-hour call, but I find it amazing to be able to communicate with an animal. You can't do it verbally, so you use body language, commands, understanding of how they react to certain situations. One of my favourite things is to work with my dog to find missing people, whether Alzheimer patients, suicidal people … there is always someone worried about the person we're looking for, and it's a great feeling to be able to help them."

Terry Higginson comes back to the house in the middle of the night to find 40 to 50 people still milling about. Crowds continue to pour down the street and to the house. Some bring their dogs.

"Here's my dog — he can help search for the little boy."

"My dog — he knows how to find people."

"No, I'm sorry, but you can't," Terry says firmly. "It contaminates the area for me. Thank you for offering, but your dog has no background in searching and I need you to take him away."

"They're not trained search dogs," Terry later explains. "People think that just because they are dogs, they can search."

Terry now has to rest Dar. He also needs to get together with the official search team and update them on his progress. He sees that the Red Cross has arrived, that more people keep coming; volunteers keep returning for water and rest.

Terry goes out into the night again. First he searches once more near the front lawn of the house, and then he conducts a more detailed investigation of the area where a creek runs through. It's a patch of ground that's very wet — like a bog. An hour passes, and another. He finds nothing.

For the other SAR team members the night also passes without clues of any kind. Between five and six in the morning, they start to return to the command post. All are exhausted. Each shift will last 12 hours. After that, other searchers will be brought in to take over from the first group.

In the early hours of the morning, before faint streaks in the sky herald the dawn of a new day, Stephen calls in two other search teams.

"There are 12 other teams altogether, and each one has over 550 volunteers," he explains. "All are trained in SAR. I call on the four closest teams and put them on standby because I think I might need their help. I ask can they get here by 7:30. They call their members and arrange to get them to the site."

By eight in the morning, amid the rustling of the woods and loud birdsong, another pleasant warm day had dawned. But below the sunny surface lies a sorrowful scene. Here, on a small dead end street outside Fredericton, someone turns on a radio; news of war, hurricanes, and floods spill from it — no sign of any of that here. The most important topic in these parts is a little boy who has been lost in a vast and lonely forest where paths lead every which way. Everyone here understands the little boy's fear. Can relate to his pain and sense of being abandoned so much more easily than to the misery of strangers on other continents where catastrophe seems a continual state of affairs.

No one has slept — not the family, the neighbours, the exhausted search team members, or the extra 50 searchers at the site. Some of the original SAR members — many of them cut by stinging nettles and bruised by low-hanging branches — have stayed. Others have gone home. Because of their lack of success at finding any clues, Terry decides that an aerial search is needed, and calls for a helicopter from the RCMP.

None are available. He approaches the Department of National Defence and asks for the use of their chopper. This time he meets with success. By nine, it's droning over the tops of the trees. Terry then returns to the woods once more with Dar. An hour passes, and another. Eleven o'clock: soon it will be midday. As the search proceeds, anxiety and fear for the little boy grow. Will they *ever* find him? If and when they do, will the child be alive — or dead? A frantic mother and grandmother are sobbing on the steps of their home. The child's uncle, tight-lipped and silent, tirelessly follows the SAR members about. But they have been this way before. They've fought with these same trees and with this dense undergrowth. They've called to Ritchie until their voices are hoarse. So far, there's been nothing. No little boy walking down the road or out of the forest.

"Hey, did you hear something? What was that?" A faint sound is heard, and everyone stops. In excitement, many voices call out. All wait.

A tiny voice answers. Energized, the group thrashes through the trees in the direction of the sound. Arms and legs shove through brambles and dense overhanging branches. Searchers push deeper in the woods. There, at the base of a tree, is a small boy. He lies curled up with a kitten and a stuffed toy in his arms. He's only 600 metres from his home.

Robert D., a neighbour, is the first to see the tiny figure curled up beneath an overhanging branch.

"Who are you?" the boy asks. "I won't come out until you give me your name."

Robert fights his way toward him. He's yelling and shaking. "That kid, he's asking for our names!" he says in amazement. "He says he won't come out until we give them. I can't believe we've found him! I've got an eight-year-old boy, so this hits very close to home. What a relief he hasn't been kidnapped. We're like one big family when it comes to things like this — we all feel it."

Ritchie has suffered nothing more than shock, confusion, and a few bug bites.

Why didn't he answer to the calls to him?

"He could have been asleep, or too afraid to answer, not knowing who was calling him," Stephen says.

"Yes, it's typical of young kids that they don't respond when you call," Terry says. "They're often afraid of being in trouble and not sure what will happen to them."

Ritchie is very glad to be home, although surprised to see so many strangers at his house. He becomes subdued. He explains he'd gone looking for his kitten. He'd followed her deeper and deeper into the woods. He says his grandfather once told him to stay put under a tree if he ever got lost in the woods.

"I wasn't scared," he says bravely. "I used my stuffed animal as a pillow and sort of made a bed to lie down in. I found a branch that hung down over me, and I held Tinker in my arms …" His eyes brighten as he says, "I met a bear, and I had to punch him in the nose … then a fox came after me and I tripped it up!"

"It's the most wonderful feeling in the world," exclaims Susie, and she reaches out her arms for her child.

"Now we got our lives back," said Gwen.

"So often search and rescue people are confronted at the end of their search by death and mutilation," said Stephen. "But not this time. This was perfect."

More than 100 people had helped in this lengthy search, one that included the York-Sunbury, Hoyt, Tri-County, Carleton, River Valley, and Charlotte County SAR organizations, the RCMP, the Red Cross, the Department of National Defence, the Maryland Volunteer Fire Department, as well as friends, relatives, and neighbours.

"It's always a very good feeling to find someone and get them back to their family," Terry says. "While there is a satisfied sense when you catch a person who has wronged someone else, this has an added dimension — doing something for another person who feels devastated and helpless because they're missing their loved one."

Stephen Moore says of his involvement with volunteer search and rescue work: "When you are involved in it, you're always very focused and anxious; your adrenaline pumps and a sense of urgency drives you. Family and neighbours come to you begging for information and help — but you're the one who needs the information! Our York-Sunbury group was formed 21 years ago after an incident where the RCMP needed searchers to help locate a missing person. We got a group together, the first group in the province, and here we are all these years later."

Terry explains that police like to maintain close links with the local SAR volunteer group. Working closely together has promoted a good relationship between them.

⠀⠀⠀⠀⠀⠀⠀⠀⠀⠀⠀⠀⠀⠀⠀⠀⠀⠀⠀⠀⠀⠀⠀⠀⠀|||||||||||||||||

Dar was retired in the fall of 2004. Corporal Terry Higginson obtained a young dog called Nick in his place and trained him. In January 2006, Nick graduated from the RCMP Police Dog Service Training Centre in Innisfail, Alberta, and man and dog continue to work together

RCMP Corporal Terry Higginson with his search dog, Dar.

to this day.

In 2006, Corporal Higginson was transferred from Fredericton, New Brunswick, to Courtenay, British Columbia. Dar remained with his family as their pet from the date of his retirement, until January 2008 when he became ill and passed away. Terry, his wife, and two sons miss him very much. His portrait is displayed throughout their house, his body donated to a highly specialized research team at the British Columbia Institute of Technology. The team of scientists there is currently conducting research with police service dogs in an effort to understand more about them. It is an area of research that has not been widely explored before in Canada. Terry is happy to know that Dar continues to help others, even after his passing.

Note: The names of the young boy and his family have been changed to protect their privacy.

8 A Navy Diver in the Afghan Desert

2007–2008, Sperwan Ghar, Afghanistan

The time is 4:45 a.m. and the sun is not yet up. With no further use for sleep — even though he hasn't had much — Navy diver Darrell Colwell slides out of a narrow cot in the cubbyhole he calls home. This temporary abode is in a Kandahar Air Force building in Afghanistan. It's a room so small he can touch both walls with outstretched arms. He has little personal stuff in it, just some books he likes to read, and a picture of his family — this is all.

He jumps into his combats — Army-issued underwear, khaki-coloured fatigues and boots — and runs downstairs to the computer room and lab. Before settling down to finish an investigative report from yesterday's incident, he quickly scans emails from home: one from his wife, and others from his three sons. But there's no time to reply as a report comes in that very instant — something about an explosion. Darrell and his team are immediately put on standby. He waits. Further information will arrive any second to tell him where his group will meet, and where they will be deployed.

This Navy diver is in the middle of the Afghan desert, his skills and expertise in bomb disposal and explosives urgently needed. His specific qualifications and experience were exactly what the Combined Explosives Exploitation Cell (CEEC) were looking for. He grabs his fly-

FASCINATING FACT
Navy Divers in the Afghanistan Desert

Based on their qualifications, divers are sent to help disarm and investigate improvised explosive devices, (IEDs). These are the biggest killers of Canadian troops. To date, 83 soldiers have died, over half from explosives and roadside bombs. The threat to the troops is so great that 29.6 million dollars will be spent on new heavy detection and route clearing systems using mine-detecting armoured vehicles — the Husky, Buffalo, and Cougar. Four teams will be fully operational by the end of 2007. A significant number of Canadian demolition experts in Afghanistan are Navy divers.

Training to Join the Troops

The same mission-specific instruction is given for all soldiers deploying to Afghanistan, whether infantry or engineers. But Navy divers have to acquire new skills to work with their army counterparts: Training in driving and commanding the crew who operate the Bison troop carriers in which they travel; learning how to operate in convoys; how to work in tandem with infantry and Quick Reaction Force teams to cordon off areas where roadside bombs are suspected; and how to deploy from their Bisons and take robots with them to inspect suspicious devices, then transmit the video images to team members.

Many instant decisions must be made: what methods should they use to make them safe? Or should they simply blow them up? They must learn how to reconstruct bombs to understand how they were made, and with what, to better counter them in the future.

Navy teams are stretched thin because of this mission. The pool of divers from which to draw has just 120 individuals in all of Canada.

away kit that contains everything he needs to do the job — a kit that's always ready to go. He checks the operation of his C-8 rifle, and over a bulletproof vest he pulls on a tactical one with many pockets. This is where he puts bullets and first-aid kits. He grabs his helmet and races to the airport tarmac. The five members of his team will investigate a United States Hummer vehicle that has been blown up on a desert road.

Once finished, they'll stay to clear the whole area, even while possibly under fire from the Taliban: Enemy forces are circling.

Knowing the temperature will quickly reach 45 degrees Celsius, each team member checks his water supply. As more information trickles in, thoughts go out to the men blown out of their vehicle.

"What about the guys who were in it?" Darrell asks.

"Thrown out, miraculously unhurt, thank God! The two got up and walked away with little more than bumps and bruises — they're in the hospital at the Kandahar Air Field."

Darrell sighs; such a relief not to be going to a more gruesome scene. Already he's sweating in the heat and once more checks his backpack for water supplies. On the tarmac, he stares at the Blackhawk helicopter as its rotors start turning. What a monster aircraft! He gazes up at it in awe. He's even more impressed when he gets inside and supposes it's because he's new to the whole Afghan scene. Today the team has an Apache as escort, a type of helicopter a little like a gunship. It will follow them. In battle it can do better than they can! A 25-minute flight in the Blackhawk takes them to a deserted compound called Sperwan Ghar.

"As we get closer, we're told the enemy forces are closing in on the place where we're headed," Darrell says. "This really gets the adrenaline running! Whatever we have to do, it will have to be quick.

Photo courtesy of Darrell Colwell.

Aerial view of the countryside around Kandahar, Afghanistan.

"We land at a spot in the desert near a rise, and jump to the ground. First thing we do is put on goggles, then a scarf over our faces. The Blackhawk's rotors kick up the dust until I can scarcely see my hand when I stretch my arm in front of me.

"The loadmaster gives exit orders. We grab our equipment, jump out of the way of the rotors and go down on one knee — it's a sign to the pilot that he can take off. We cover our faces and the Blackhawk takes off. Dust is everywhere. It's a very fine powder like I imagine moon dust to be — very soft. Put your foot on it and it puffs out in the air around you.

"We are greeted by members of the United States Task Force; the ones who suffered the strike on the ground. We're loaded into their Hummers, and driven 500 metres to the control point. We approach a rise in the dusty plateau and the armoured vehicle stops. Just 100 metres ahead of us lies the wreckage of the blown-up Hummer. From this range we can see it, blasted by improvised explosive devices [IEDs], and totally destroyed. Now a million bits of chrome and steel lie glinting in the desert sand. Scattered all about are damaged explosives, grenades, and weapons of all kinds. The EOD team declares the ground clear and we get to work at once, gathering it all into a pile and blowing it all up to make sure it's totally disabled. The sound is like that of a single clap of thunder, the spectacle like the fireworks and explosions you see as special effects in movies.

"Then we get down to the business of investigating the cause of the IED strike. We start collecting everything that's salvageable from the device so we can take it to the lab for analyzing. First we'll try to rebuild it; to find out what materials and substances were used, learn how it was put together, and how it was detonated.

"I'll search for and collect forensic evidence — like fingerprints and hair — anything that will help us put together a profile of who might have done this. Urgency drives us. Enemy forces are close, and getting closer. We're in Sperwan Ghar, an area already overrun by the Taliban. They want it for its strategic importance — for a stronghold. Our Forces want it for the same reason. It sits on a rise overlooking surrounding countryside, with the town of Panjaway in the distance. We are ordered to secure it by this very nightfall!

"The drumming heat is insistent. We sweat. We're bent over, with dust in every pore, even though we're covered up. Three long, tedious hours pass while we clear the entire area of possible mines and explosive devices. To the delight of the Task Force commander, we finish it all and set up camp for the night. Because we're in control of the area I'm feeling a little more comfortable and grab a moment to look over the landscape: mud dwellings scattered about, all divided by the same mud walls, startling patches of bright green — I learn that these cultivated rectangles are marijuana fields with plants that grow up to six feet tall! Beyond, and all about, the desert seems to stretch empty to the horizon.

"Darkness falls. The night is black and full of threat. We camp in an abandoned schoolhouse. Still wearing our combat clothes, we drop onto a concrete floor to sleep. Little sleep comes: One eye open and one closed — we're watchful — and not alone. Crawling all over us, in eyes and ears and everywhere else, is an army of big black ants. We swat and flick them away, but they don't harm us, and in the end just have to put up with them; to put up with it all. Eyes closed again. Some of us fall into exhausted sleep — but not for long. After exactly an hour we're jerked awake by the sudden and nightmarish sound of gunfire. We

Soldiers patrol the rugged terrain near Sperwan Ghar in armoured vehicles.

Photo courtesy of the Department of National Defence.

jump up, grab our rifles, and immediately and take up position. The Task Force commander calls in air support. The blasting of guns and rockets seems never to stop. It comes closer; the Taliban is closing in. Ear-piercing rocket fire keeps up until dawn when we have a tiny feeling of relief: In the light of day we know the enemy will slink off.

"The sun is up and the heat drills through us. The United States Task Force commander orders us to sweep the road right around the hill, to clear it of mines and explosives — on this very road an Afghan National Army soldier just had his foot blown off. The area is prominent — on a hill with an advantageous view all around. If we can clear it, we will have secured it for the combined Armed Forces. The work is critical. It's gruelling. All of us are exhausted, and lack of sleep hasn't helped.

"A relentless sun and its blistering heat crush down. Sweat forms fast and drips off us like we'd just run a marathon. We find the work very hard, and every second we have to be extremely vigilant. A pervasive sense of fear haunts us because our enemy is close. What you do is push it into the background of your thoughts. In fact, you actually feel calm; you never waver. Anxiety doesn't creep over you when you're busy defusing bombs and mines — only after it's all over. At the time you're so focused on what you're doing there's no time to feel anything — except the adrenaline still pumping. It keeps racing for long afterwards.

"The EOD finds landmines on the road and blows them up in place. Every second we're being extremely vigilant — we have to be! By late afternoon we've cleared the entire road around the hill. We can sit down at last.

"Our commander tells us we've done a great job. Because we managed to clear the whole area, it has become a forward operating base for our troops. We've taken it from the Taliban!

"Back in the cubbyhole, on my bunk bed, dark thoughts let loose. My mind wanders over the past two or three days. What could have happened out there? *My* foot could have blown off. *I* could have been blown up. What if I'd missed a mine? Stepped on one? When I think like this, I remind myself that what I'm doing is good. It's helpful and useful. I'm clearing out mines. I'm saving lives and limbs."

॥॥॥॥॥॥॥॥॥॥॥॥॥॥

Darrell's first tour of duty in Afghanistan came after September 11, 2001. His team's task was to search for terrorists on board ships and to hunt for drug smugglers. A second tour began in July 2006, and finished in March 2007. On this second tour he found himself the lone Canadian, invited by the United States Army to be part of the Combined Explosive Cell in Kandahar. The scope of his qualifications was all-encompassing, his skills in critical demand.

"I volunteered because people like me were needed," he said. "I had all the qualifications required — not many people do. In fact it's rare to have them all. I trained for everything I possibly could, because when I was put in charge of the Explosives Ordnance Disposal section — when I'm put in charge of any operation — I feel it my responsibility to know as much as I can about it. I never want to be in a position where I don't have all the information and skills that could possibly be needed. It's about the kind of person I am: I have to do things to the very best of my ability; to know I'm master of all everything that might arise." He pauses, and then adds, "It's also because I'm fulfilling my career, putting to good use all my extensive and expensive training."

"People ask why I put myself in greater danger than I'm already in. They want to know because they think my work as a diver disposing of bombs and explosives is already dangerous. And of course they ask, "Why does a Navy diver go to the Afghan desert?" Well, you have to deal with what's on the surface, as well as what's under the water. We are bomb disposal and explosives proficient: It doesn't matter whether in the water, or above it.

"People in the Army tend to go away a lot — like every six months. They come home for six months. They train for six months and go away again. We're losing people in Afghanistan. Some are not coming home at all. I feel that if I take up a position it will allow one person to come home and stay with his family for longer. It's also a good feeling to put all my training into use — I know where my salary is coming from!

"There are a number of Canadian demolition experts in Afghanistan that are people like me — Navy divers," he says. "I have to say, I think the world of the Army. When I'm singled out for recognition, I try to make sure everyone knows I represent many others who also take big risks, who are probably more deserving than me. They sacrifice time with family, and personal comfort. They put themselves in danger."

FASCINATING FACT
Navy Clearance Diving

This name arose during wartime when one country would mine the harbours of another. Divers were sent in to clear them and make them safe by getting rid of mines or explosives that had been laid.

This remains their primary job because the threat is always there. For this they train continuously, but they also train for much more — ship repairs, underwater welding, maintenance of equipment and diving gear, as well as the training of Military and Clearance divers all across Canada, combat training, and Search and Rescue. Not the least of these is underwater welding. This has become important on many occasions, particularly after the Swiss Air Disaster off Nova Scotia, and the floods in New Orleans after Hurricane Katrina.

There are only 120 people in the Mine Counter-Measure team and its members never cease practising getting rid of mines.

Where are the risks to ships coming into Canada, a person might ask.

"The threat is always there," Darrell says. "It cannot be overlooked. All ships coming into Victoria Harbour are searched by underwater explosives experts. They also assist the RCMP with calls made on the island about bomb threats. It happens more than you want to know. There are pranks as well — kid stuff like Halloween, and kids getting on the Internet."

Sacrifice is an appropriate word for the work that takes place in Afghanistan. Darrell worked for the Combined Explosive Exploitation Cell in Kandahar. His team's task was to investigate all improvised explosive devices (IEDs) — *all* incidents.

Of course it was absolutely impossible to respond to all the calls. Afghanistan has many provinces under RC South, the regional command under which Darrell worked, and there were only three members in Kandahar. Calls poured in day and night — calls for help that never seemed to cease.

"We'd go from one to another. We worked 14 hours a day and more," he says. "It was very stressful the whole time. Your threshold was always heightened because you never knew what was going to happen. Everything was dangerous. Sometimes the place seemed like a vast, menacing desert; a place where anarchy ruled by night, and sometimes by day.

"This is how you lived, your adrenaline pumping furiously all the time. You were never sure you were safe. But you did know that extreme vigilance made things a little bit safer.

"The job you do — you don't think about it — at least until afterwards. While you're working, you're in an altered state of consciousness: You can do anything. Nothing else exists at the time. You focus in on this thing you must do. Only afterwards you think: Ugh! What a close call!

"The work affects us because the things we do are far outside what ordinary people can relate to; it's outside normality, not part of any society. At the time we might call it a living nightmare. Conditions are difficult, uncomfortable, unpredictable — and dangerous. We have little respite, little time for the adrenaline to subside. We live in a heightened state of awareness that only others who have been there can relate to. But one thing you do develop is bonding with your mates.

"You are not the same person as the one who left to go there. You are changed. When I got home I learned to enjoy colours — there are few in Afghanistan. I now love all the flowers at home, the vegetation, the beauty. I no longer take for granted what I have, and what's around me. Last year I planted a beautiful garden … grass … trees … I wanted to create a profusion of colours. I developed a keen appreciation for what has always been around me that's not over there.

"One day I went to the mall and sat on a bench. I felt invisible. People didn't see me because they rarely see what's around them. They don't know how lucky they are that they can just go to a mall and not worry about anything. I now appreciate freedom and the day-to-day things — I really like the day-to-day — it's important. We are free. We'll be around tomorrow. When we go out, we know we're coming home."

‖‖‖‖‖‖‖‖‖‖‖‖

As a child, Darrell had been known as a water rat, entirely at home in the watery world: In it, on it, above it. To him it was a different universe — like being in space. Most people had no access to it. This universe for him became a personal and private thing.

In his teen years he achieved a position with Team Canada's swim team. He attended international meets. Soon he was diving. Then a chosen career as a commercial diver where he could be in and under the water.

He graduated, only to find that experience was needed. There was little work. He returned to school at Seneca College in Toronto to get the experience that employers were asking for. There he met ex-Navy divers who were teaching his courses. Navy diving — this was it! At once he went off to the career centre to check it out. A mere 14 days later he was in a military boot camp in Cornwall, Nova Scotia. Included among all that he learned was training as a weapons technician.

Darrell discovered that he could not join the military as a clearance diver; he had to *re-muster*. This meant going from one trade to another; from a weapons technician to clearance diver. The training was year-long, and tough — mentally and physically strenuous. Darrell found it satisfying and rewarding — how many people could do this kind of thing? Many could not, and dropped out.

How does he feel about being in Afghanistan? The question keeps returning. Darrell answers that people with his expertise are desperately needed there, and someone has to do it. Homemade bombs are killing Canadian troops — they are the biggest threat. He adds that it is the teams — Army, Air Force, Navy — that save lives, and to him, they are all heroes.

"You do have a sense of accomplishment," he says. "You know you're helping these people. In the villages, if you could see the eyes of children when we give them soccer balls and watermelon and dolls, you wouldn't ask why we're there. You know you're there for a reason."

9 Rime of an Ancient Lifeboat Coxwain

February 21, 2001, and July 5, 1975. Louisbourg, Cape Breton

And now there came both mist and snow,
And it grew wondrous cold:
And ice, mast-high, came floating by,
As green as emerald.
   —*The Rime of the Ancient Mariner*, Samuel Taylor Coleridge

"Afterwards, this fellow comes up and he says to me, 'If my son was on your boat and something woulda happened because of the icing situation, there woulda been someone having to answer a few questions.'"

"I said to him, I said, 'it's like this: what if it was your son been on that fishing boat? What if I never went out — then who would be asking the questions?'

"The fellow couldn't answer. He had nothing to say to that. I tell you this: For me, I go out when I'm called. I do what I can to the best of my abilities, and I hope and pray to God everything will be all right. Knock on wood, I haven't lost anybody yet. But it's not to say it couldn't happen."

Wayne Dowling is an old man of the sea. For 32 years he has served as a Search and Rescue worker for the Canadian Coast Guard. The lifeboat station is perched on a rocky foreshore at Louisbourg, Cape Breton Island. When called, he sets out in his little boat to face the wrath of the Atlantic Ocean at a time when all other boats hurry in to safe harbour.

A short, stocky man with a receding hairline, Wayne has about him the look of an ancient mariner. On this 21st day of February 2001, he stands at the window of the trailer that acts as the lifeboat station. A placid North Atlantic laps gently at his feet, an ocean that right now is mostly free of ice. Wayne lifts his eyes to stare over the harbour, and beyond to the rocks that guard it. All are silhouetted in a soft morning light. It is a tranquil scene, but deceiving. Outside, an extreme cold covers all of Cape Breton Island and immobilizes the landscape into peculiar stillness.

The infamous calm before the storm, Wayne thinks. His mind drifts to other times, to storms that thrust the sea almost to the trailer door. This winter, the station has had few calls — and none today. Not many vessels,

FASCINATING FACT
How Did the Canadian Coast Guard Evolve?

The evolution of the Canadian Coast Guard is a fascinating one. In the early years of Canadian shipping, a near-total lack of safety measures existed, and a lack of concern for the well-being of sea travellers. Navigation was "by guess and by God." Crews were inexperienced and untrained. The hardships suffered by yesterday's mariners were so great that the great English sage, Samuel Johnson, once remarked that "no one would put himself onto a ship who had means enough to get himself into a jail."

If fire and storm did not immobilize a vessel, then pirates, marauders, and buccaneers would lure them to disaster. Frequent shipwrecks meant repeated heroic rescue attempts by captain and crew, by the crew of nearby ships, and by people who lived along the shores where ships foundered.

Establishing lifesaving support along Canada's extensive, sparsely populated coastlines that bordered the Atlantic, Pacific, and Arctic Oceans was a challenge to the young country. It wasn't until the 1700s, after a series of terrible shipwrecks, that the government felt pressured to provide lifeboat stations. To give help to shipwrecked mariners in Eastern Canada, it established Canada's first light station on Sable Island, Nova Scotia, in 1758, another in Cape Breton in 1777, and one in St. John's, Newfoundland, in 1791.

Formal assistance to shipwrecked sailors began with specific groups of volunteers who were called "soldiers of the surf," or "storm warriors." They would often be seen pulling a wooden rowing boat to the water's edge and pulling on the oars in the thrashing seas. It wasn't until Confederation in 1867 that the federal government took over the large collection of aid systems, of lifesaving stations and any apparatus on shore that supported them. It became the Department of Marine and Fisheries' task to oversee the systems and take responsibility for Search and Rescue.

In 1936, the government passed the Department of Transportation Act to bring all the components under a single federal authority. In 1962, the fleet of vessels used in marine service was named the Canadian Coast Guard.

CCGC Spindrift *attempting to stay in lee of the* Sir William Alexander *to reduce icing, February 2001.*

apart from an occasional fishing boat, would dare venture out upon the sea in these temperatures. At four in the afternoon he closes the station, and he and the crew go home, pagers in their pockets in case of a call.

It's dinner time, around 6:00 p.m., when the Coast Guard's Rescue Co-ordination Centre in Halifax intrudes upon the Dowlings' evening.

Sixty-five-foot fishing vessel the *I.V.Y.* has radioed to say they have steering problems: they have trouble staying on course and emergency steering only. Will the lifeboat crew go out and assist.

Just another call to rescue, but what a call! And what a night! Wayne learns that the fishing boat is far out on the ocean, close to Magdalen Island of St. Pierre. This is 80 or more miles from Louisbourg. If the captain is using emergency steering "it means someone's in the back end of the boat with a tiller stick," Wayne comments. At this point, it's all he knows.

Other crew members stop what they're doing, say goodbye to their families, and race off to the station. They are Lorne Calvert, Kenny Fraser, and James Bates. They greet each other, and immediately spring to action. The *Spindrift*, their 44-foot lifeboat, must be prepared for freezing conditions and a long tow. Just 20 minutes from the time of the call and the men are on their way to the rescue of the large fishing boat.

Coastal waters are calm as they leave the station. The thermometer reads minus 50 degrees Celsius, with wind to stern — but the cabin is heated. Window panels are heated. Windshield wipers move briskly back and forth. But the chilled area around them leaves only a four-inch hole in each panel through which the pilot can see.

At the halfway point, conditions change suddenly: The sea rears itself up in spitting green fury and the lifeboat lunges as it flies over the rocking waves. Crew members give each other silent glances. There's a further 30 to 40 miles yet to travel in these conditions before they reach the stricken fishing vessel.

"The wind begins to blow like the dickens," Wayne says. "It's going to be quite a night." And so begins an ordeal of a kind the crew has seldom endured in all their years of rescue work.

Wayne feels for the fellows in trouble; he was a fisherman once, and knows what trouble is. He stands at the wheel, straining to see through the frost buildup. He rubs his hands for warmth. Ice is building up on deck and the boat is beginning to list. Winds howl. Waves slap up against the hull. Water and sea spray thrash over decks even as ice floes crunch beneath the hull. The boat increases its listing. Another hour passes, and another; it seems that no time has passed, yet unending time.

The darkness of night has long since swallowed up any glimpse of the watery landscape. A whole six hours has passed, and now, suddenly, they are upon the stricken fishing vessel. The crew cheers. In the gloom, Wayne struggles to manoeuvre the lifeboat alongside the larger one. His men are on deck — decks that are slick with ice. They grab at the railings to keep upright and on board as they prepare to throw a tow line. The sea thrusts up and sea spray blinds as one of them throws the line. It arcs up and across the howling space between the boats. Arms are outstretched as it flies across — to land right on the deck of the crippled vessel! A waiting fisherman snatches it up and immediately attaches it. Again the sound of cheering erupts. Now begins the long and crippling trek back to shore in the bitter cold. Like a tiny tugboat pulling a giant tanker to dock, the lifeboat lugs the fishing vessel toward the safety of the shore.

On the return trip, more ice builds on the lifeboat's deck and around its windshields. The seas are still high. The crew is thinking they might make it … just make it … when abruptly the lifeboat's engines stall.

What now? Something — maybe a plastic bag — has got wound around the propellers.

This is what Wayne thinks. Something's binding the propellers up tight and stalling the engines. Now they have no steering. No power.

A struggle begins that is to last two hours. Wayne pushes the engine into reverse, then forward into drive. He thrusts it back and forth, back and forth until, just as suddenly, the foreign object comes free. The engines turn over to the cheers of the crew, and the lifeboat plows ahead.

But his troubles are not over: Wayne now looks with alarm at his boat's worsening list — a list so severe that the little lifeboat is almost on its side. He and his crew are in immediate danger. He tries to reach Sydney's Coast Guard radio station to ask for help. Sydney can hear him, but Wayne doesn't know it because his radio is not receiving properly. With increasing frustration he tries to make himself heard. His lifeboat is now almost completely iced up and lists at an angle of 20 to 30 degrees. He has slowed to a crawl; nothing to do now but send his three crewmen on deck with wooden mallets to try to clear it.

The crew, wearing their bulky orange survival suits, bang their mallets on the frozen surface. The work is treacherous: decks are slippery, and slope steeply. The cold is bitter. The men, like bizarre apparitions from some alien place, smash up the ice and remove it. Chunks have formed on the water like thick islands. They begin to surround the little lifeboat that is still 26 miles from home.

The *Spindrift* struggles on in silence. Fear is in the hearts of her crew. They are afraid for themselves, and for the fishing vessel. *But what's this?* — A shape looms up ahead and a loud cheer erupts. It's the Coast Guard's icebreaker *Sir William Alexander*. It glides out of the gloom and comes alongside.

"We're doing all right," Wayne radios laconically, "but we'd like you to go ahead and take some of the heat off us. We'd like for you to bear the brunt of the storm. We'll ride behind you."

The icebreaker does just this: It forges a path for the lifeboat through a rough sea of ice and storm. As noon approaches they see Louisbourg looming ahead.

The crew of the lifeboat has endured nine hours of towing in the bitter sea. Together, the icebreaker and the lifeboat approach the harbour shoal buoy. As the *Sir William Alexander* is no longer needed, it stands down and continues on to Sydney to resume its icebreaking work in the harbour.

Wayne begins shortening up the tow lines. "We have two big lines together — one of them 600 feet, the other 900," he says. "Fifteen hundred feet altogether. There's a shackle between the two. But one line must have taken the other line down when we were backing up. I'm about to go ahead when one gets stuck in the propeller. I'm stalled. I try to tow the *I.V.Y.* with one engine, but can't do it. There's no manoeuvring. I get on the radio to the *Sir William Alexander*

Photo courtesy of DFO and the Canadian Coast Guard.

Canadian Coast Guard ice-breaking ships on standby for Search and Rescue.

and ask them to please turn back and help me — and I'm only half a mile from shore! The thing is, with one propeller and one engine working, I'm steering and handling the boat myself. But as soon as I take the fishing boat in tow — and because of his rudder angle to starboard — he can't steer. I can't manoeuvre. The fishing boat just keeps going around in circles."

Wayne lets the line go and asks the *Sir William Alexander* to tow the fishing boat into Louisbourg's harbour. When the icebreaker gets as close as its size allows, another fishing vessel takes over and tows it to dock.

"First time in my life I ever had a rope in my [propeller] blade," Wayne says.

For this rescue, Wayne Dowling receives the Commissioner's Commendation "in recognition of your outstanding efforts … [Y]our professionalism and dedication exemplify the finest tradition of the Canadian Coast Guard."

||||||||||||||||||

A man and his crew have little fear of heavy ice buildup on the decks of their lifeboat to the point of its capsizing, have little fear of perishing in the extreme cold of icy seas — but they fear a summer storm.

> But soon I heard the dash of oars
> I heard the pilot's cheer;
> My head was turned perforce away
> And I saw a boat appear!
>   —*The Rime of the Ancient Mariner,* Samuel Taylor Coleridge

It was July 5, 1975. This was no ordinary storm — *Never seen the likes of it before,* local people say, their voices full of awe as they talk about the big seas that thrashed the coast. Seas that swamped the government dock and washed over part of their town on that day the little lifeboat went out to rescue a fishing boat lost off the coast. Winds blew up to 60 or 70 knots, and torrents of rain and thunderstorms punished the east coast of Cape Breton Island.

A local fishing vessel was out long-line fishing in that storm. Its engines failed. The pilot's father went out with the Coast Guard's lifeboat crew to bring them in. The seas were huge and seething. *Would any of them return?* the people asked, their eyes raised to the heavens.

"When I left that day, light winds were called for; the outlook was good," said George Le Moine, owner of the fishing boat *Lady Marilyn.* "Lovely day when we went out. We put out our gear — about eight miles of it — long-lining for cod. We set our lines at night and we'd haul them in next morning — you have to let it soak awhile. Our three-man crew had begun at daybreak and it took them the whole day to get it in. Everything was going well when one of the crew heard a radio broadcast from Sydney radio. They had revised the weather forecast."

George didn't pay much attention. "When they change a forecast, they just step it up a bit," he said. *And this was July,* he might have added, *not a time of the year when you expect high winds and storms.* "Then we heard another forecast — winds to blow up to 15 to 20 knots," he said. "Next thing they're telling us it's up to 30. When they call for high winds like this, you don't take any chances. You head back in. The wind was hitting elsewhere — we could see it.

"We anchored out our lines and marked them with a buoy so we could retrieve them some other time. Then we prepared to head in — all of the vessels were starting to get in. You could see the wind coming — 50 to 60 miles an hour from the southeast. We got closer to shore where the sea depth is only

> ## FASCINATING FACT
> ### Risks to a Rescuer
>
> Today, the general fear of liability, and the costs associated with it, often stops people from going to the aid of others. But the Coast Guard does not restrain its Search and Rescue workers by keeping them on shore while storms rage and people perish on the seas. The people in the Rescue Centre control rooms know that, in spite of sophisticated technology that allows them a virtual presence at the scene of a shipwreck, they can never really understand the conditions. They cannot know exactly what the risks are to the rescuers. They have deep respect for the experience and judgment of their frontline crews and allow them to make their own decisions about what risks they will take.

about 30 to 50 fathoms — not a lot of water — and it's much rougher. It's always rougher the closer you get in. The wind was behind us and the seas got up to 30- and 40-foot waves. Our boat was only 30 feet [in length]. I had to slow her down. But she tossed around so much she stirred up my fuel tanks — stirred up dirt or rust or anything that was in the tank, and it plugged up the line. I tried to clear it, but I ended up twisting the fuel line clean from the tank. No way I could fix this."

In this freak storm, winds shifted and now blew from the southwest. It did nothing to improve conditions. George tried to guide his boat away from shore, then to run parallel to it. But high winds and tide fast blew him straight toward it. Worried now, he threw over his anchor. He threw the trawl anchors as well — seven in total. Like a leering devil, the coast of Cape Breton loomed, jagged and menacing. George saw other fishing boats running to the safety of the shore, among them his own father in a 60-foot vessel.

Feeling very much at the mercy of a violent and shallow sea, and very nervous now, George radioed the Coast Guard.

"We're about dead in the water," he told the Regional Control Centre in Halifax. "Fuel line's off, and we have no power."

George's father heard this broadcast, turned around, and headed straight back out to sea to try to help rescue his son. At the same moment, the Coast Guard lifeboat steered into the storm to try to help the fishing boat.

"I had the throttle wide open, gave it whatever it could do," said Wayne Dowling, coxswain of the lifeboat. "I had the engines right to the floor of our boat. That guy was soon to be up on the rocks."

On the shore, and all over the government dock, people came to watch the drama of a freak summer storm — to see waves tossing right over the lighthouse and making it invisible.

Never seen such big seas, the locals said, awestruck. They saw that the government wharf, too, lay completely covered in water. They watched the little lifeboat and its crew set out on the water, a blip upon a thrashing sea. Heard how its engines roared, and how it seemed to jump right out of the water.

"That fishing boat in trouble — it stood four miles out from shore," Wayne said. "But when we got to it, it was just 200 feet from the rocks — very close. In big trouble, it was. We made it out to them fast as we could."

George, frightened for himself and his crew, and worried about his father, felt an even greater fear as one of the crew of the lifeboat stood up to throw a heaving line.

"They had to get very close to us because the line had to be hauled in by hand," he said. "With the waves so high, I got scared they were going to crash down and go right through us. One boat stood on the crest of a wave 30 or 40 feet above, the other in its trough. The wave could hit our boat and push it to one side. We tried to go head-on through the waves. We looked up at the lifeboat from very far below — looked up, and saw one giant green fist of a wave that could knock us sideways, a wave that could come right through us. That lifeboat crew, they had to watch they didn't hit us, had to watch out to avoid all our anchors. At the same time, to get the tow line aboard us."

Crew member William Hunt, drenched and buffeted by wind and waves as he slithered about the bow of the lifeboat, waited for that split second when the lifeboat was roughly on the same level as the fishing vessel, when one was on the upswing and the other on the downswing.

It was only then he had a chance to throw — and it was but one chance. If he missed, he wouldn't get another; the fishing boat would strike the rocks. Out of the corner of his eye he saw them: jagged, rocky outcrops that loomed ever closer, their vessels on a forward gallop toward this terrible horizon.

William made a monkey fist (the end knot for a heaving line). He waited, and then threw.

"We got him first throw!" exalted the crew. A *Lady Marilyn* crew member grabbed the small line and pulled it in.

"They were just holding on for dear life," Wayne said. "If we hadn't made good on that first throw, their boat would have been in the surf, and we couldn't have got into it — not where they were. Very lucky for him, it was. We were out on the sea where the waves stood at 30 to 40 feet, and I was afraid of pulling the fishing boat under while we were towing. I was really afraid this time," he said gravely. "I'm climbing a wave — like scaling a mountaintop. I'm cutting down the power so I don't drag him under by pulling his bow down. He could have had all his windows smashed out … his boat could've sunk right under. And I had to keep my engines running at half-speed just to keep head to the wind."

The captain of the *Lady Marilyn*, once the tow line was attached, had to abandon all his anchors — anchors that hadn't even hooked the ocean bottom, so fast was the drift. He marked them with a buoy so that he could get them at a later date.

The lifeboat first pulled the fishing boat off the land a little, then towed it out from shore. On board the *Lady Marilyn*, George worried that the brute force of wind and wave would pull the cleat right off his boat — or off the lifeboat. "With that much wind and that much strain … if you think you're going to be hit hard, you slow your boat right down. But I had no control over that once I was under tow. We had to take everything that was coming back at us: no steering, no engine power. One of my crew stood on the north side of the wheelhouse. I stood on the other. The wind just picked him up and threw him right across the deck. He landed in a chair, and he crushed it.

"The wind — never seen anything like it in all the years I've been at the station," Wayne said again. "I couldn't see the lighthouse when I was coming in, even when I was close up."

Photo courtesy of DFO and the Canadian Coast Guard.

Air and marine units work closely together to perform dangerous rescues over open water. Here the two perform a training exercise.

The coxswain now had trouble pulling the fishing boat in because of winds that blew straight to shore. Unable to tow directly into the harbour, he had to beat a path up — offshore — and to the left of the harbour, keeping the wind to portside.

"We had to go in at an angle, run up off the shore, then turn to the shore," he said. "We were afraid of capsizing. Afraid of towing; of having the heavy seas beat the wheelhouse off the boat we were towing."

He mused afterward that perhaps he and his crew should not have gone out that time, should not have been in that storm. Could he have refused? When a call to a rescue appears as a potentially risky one, he asks his crew if they are willing to go out. Invariably they answer yes. If one refuses, another can always be found. But this has never happened: No one has ever refused — Wayne has never refused.

"Some days I think I will just pack my bag and go get a land job," he said. "But here I am, still doing a job I love. "You get an adrenaline rush — know what I mean? You say to yourself, *maybe I can go and save this person*. You get worked up, your adrenaline pumps and you just go. Everything worked out fine; I'd go back and do it again."

Wayne Dowling and his crew — William Hunt and Harold Fudge — received personal commendation from the commissioner of the Canadian Coast Guard for their efforts in this rescue.

"I was most impressed with the report of your valiant effort ... when the three of you saved three lives ... under particularly difficult conditions," he wrote. "Your unflinching devotion to duty and excellent seamanship was well demonstrated by that fact that the lifeboat set out in 60-knot winds and high seas ... such exemplary service prompts the wholehearted admiration of your colleagues within the Canadian Coast Guard, and commands the esteem of the seafaring community at large.... My personal commendation for a job well done."

||||||||||||||||||

Wayne Dowling lives with his wife, close to the Mira River, near New Boston. He has a son, a daughter, and three grandchildren. Clocking in at 32 years of service with the Coast Guard, he is one of the oldest Search and Rescue workers in eastern Canada.

10 "I Seen a Ghost"

September 19, 2004, Bonavista, Newfoundland

I like being a service person because it all comes down to honour. Like, every day when I put on my uniform, a Canadian flag on my left shoulder, I know that I stand for something. I know I'm going to help, to be at the beck and call of others, and serve them.
— Norm Penny, SAR Tech

Young Norm Penny relates his story.

I'm relaxing one Sunday evening. I pick up the phone to call my brother, but only get in a few words on how things have been when my cell phone goes off. All I hear of Captain Scott Tromp's message is "Men abandoning ship. Will be in life raft within minutes — see you at work."

Well, okay! I've been in the Army, but here I'm the new kid who's just arrived at 103 Search and Rescue Squadron. All I've got under my belt is a string of stand-down missions and a dry spell; only one real rescue. I need a good one — soon.

Well, I got one now. I stick my head out the door. Oh man! Winds are howling and the trees are whipping around — must be the tail of Hurricane Ivan — real nasty stuff; a black night coming down fast.

Soon I get more information about the fishing boat *Ryan's Commander.* It has capsized off Bonavista and is sinking. Its six fishermen are right now clinging to a life raft. Heck, no one should be out in that kind of weather, I mean, we're talking about a tropical storm. We're talking about winds gusting and a sea state of 11 metres — as high as three- and four-storey houses! About rain coming down that could drown us all.

I race off to the squadron and meet up with the rest of our team: Flight Engineer Master Corporal Ab Pierce, Captain Scott Tromp, and Captain Mike Mondry. Sergeant Derek Rogers is the senior Search and Rescue (SAR) team leader. We're all there listening to Captain Tromp give us the official report. "The fishing boat called *Ryan's Commander* is shipwrecked off Bonavista and its crew has abandoned ship," he says. "Last report says they are climbing into their life raft."

As the captain briefs us, I notice daylight has fled and the night has come down on us. It's hard to tell right now if the weather will stay the same, or get a whole lot worse.

We get busy preparing our gear for the mission while the Cormorant helicopter is prepared to fly us to the sinking boat: It has to be completely filled up with gas, and we have to strip it down — something we do when we go out to sea. For some reason today, we decide to keep all the gear. Then there is the Hercules aircraft — it will fly overhead and stay with us throughout the rescue operation — standard procedure for a rescue over water.

The time is 2000 hours. We're ready. We should make it to the coast in half an hour. Just 20 minutes after the call, we're airborne in the Cormorant. The Hercules aircraft is ready to follow us.

Man, it's a rough ride. We're really getting buffeted as we prepare our gear. The night is black. We're into a bad storm and the chopper

> ## FASCINATING FACT
> ### Stripping Down an Aircraft
>
> Stripping down the helicopter prior to a rescue mission: removing all equipment that is not strictly necessary for the rescue in question.

Photo courtesy of DFO and the Canadian Coast Guard.

The Sir Wilfrid Laurier *Coast Guard ship setting out on a rescue mission with a Canadian Forces helicopter for backup.*

is flying sideways as it fights the wind. But we're not thinking about that; we're busy looking at all the possible scenarios we could face with men in the sea, or with men in a life raft. Okay, what do we need? — dive gear and dry suits of course — for who would ever willingly throw themselves into the freezing North Atlantic without them? It's May, but the average water temperature is only two degrees.

So, what else do we need? Flashlights, tanks, and the rescue basket — a thing like a metal cage that can hold two people.

As we fly, we go over and over all the possibilities and all the drills. Half an hour later we've arrived at the last known position of *Ryan's Commander*.

Hey, we've got a contact at our two o'clock! We turn the spotlight on, trying to see what it is. It's a marker. And within seconds a new contact comes at the same location. A flare goes up — and so does my heart! Okay, this is it — we've found them. We have survivors! We're fully dressed and ready to hoist these people from their raft. Our drills and all our training kick in. We're not going to jump, because it's not possible at night and in a sea state this bad the crew might not get back the person who jumped. What we're going to do is use a hoist.

Very quickly the hoist is attached to SAR Tech Derek Rogers, and then to the chopper. Because Derek is our team leader, he'll go down first. He's ready to be lowered. Before he goes down he briefs us about what's going to happen.

"I'll be hoisted down to the shipwrecked sailors," he says. "One by one I'll try to get them up with the rescue collar. First I'll go for anyone seriously injured, and next, anyone without life-supporting equipment — like a guy without a survival suit."

All the while I'm listening, I'm keeping an anxious eye on the shoreline and the cliffs; they're awfully close and they seem to be getting closer all the time.

Derek has dropped down. After a few minutes he's got his head inside the raft. He uses hand signals to tell us all the men are alive, but only two have immersion suits — not four, as we'd been told. Those guys have been in the raft for about an hour and none of them are in good condition. We learn that they're cold, some are hypothermic, and all of them are terrified. One can't swim. This is not good. Derek has just enough time to decide who he'll take first, when his hoist fails!

We try to yank him up but he gets dragged about in the water between the chopper and the raft. We can see what's happening because the helicopter's hover lights are shining on the water. We pull him. First we get him out of the raft, and then pull him away from it.

Derek finally shows up in the chopper doorway. Hey, but he's coming in sideways! This is not normal. We usually present ourselves squarely, our shoulders facing the SAR Tech. We all stare. Our team leader has been banged up pretty bad. He's hardly conscious and looks like he's severely injured. His suit has been ripped open by the hoist hook, and it leaves a six-inch gash that has cut open his stomach. At first he just lies there, drifting in and out of consciousness. This is our senior person, and he's badly injured. He certainly won't be going down again. After a few moments he rouses himself to brief the aircraft commander, and it's only then he takes a look at his injuries. He sees the big tear in his suit and that he's bleeding from his chest. But when he looks up, he has fire in his eyes and an edge to his voice.

"Look, we can still get a few of these guys up before their raft gets blown onto the rocks," he says urgently. Then he looks at me and gives the thumbs-up. "It's you, buddy. But I'll be looking after things from up here."

My heart starts racing. Okay, it's my turn to go down. I want to go for sure and do my job, but I'm nervous. I've just seen my boss, and what happened to him. It's going to be hard. Not only this, we're running out of time for those guys. Maybe we can get even half of them up. One thing for sure is, if we don't do something soon, they'll all die. We've got a chance to get them before they hit the rocks. We have to try.

I walk to the aircraft door and stick my head out. Nothing but blackness; nothing but a howling wind. Suddenly I see a green light, then a flare near the water. The pilot keeps the helicopter flying overhead, and now suddenly I can see it — wow, how that raft is moving! It's rolling hard and pitching sideways in the waves. And it's getting closer to the rocks all the time.

I'm being hoisted down. Next thing I know the wind hits me, then I'm in the water. It's wild! My mask goes sideways with the very first wave that hits me. The ocean is a black monster that's crashing me about.

I swim as fast as I can toward the raft, dragging a cable with me. The raft has been lit up by the chopper — great! I get to it, and now can see the poor fishermen — all of them but two are without survival suits. They're the ones who will have to be brought up first. Already I can see that one of them is in poor shape. All he's wearing is a cotton shirt and jeans. I talk reassuringly to him as I put a rescue collar about him and hook him up. Then I pull him toward me, and into the water. When he realizes he has no flotation he thinks he's sinking and starts struggling wildly. Then he panics. Oh my God, he's pulling me down! He's pushing me down and using me as his flotation. He's going to drown me! Now he's knocked my mask off. He's knocked my breathing apparatus out of my mouth. He's on top of my head and I'm swallowing water … I can't stay above it … I can't breathe … can't breathe …

Somehow I manage to get my flotation device activated. It pops open. It gives me extra buoyancy but restricts my breathing. I've got too much equipment on me — but I need all of it for this kind of rescue.

With my thumb I signal to the operator to hoist both of us up. I can feel the cable pulling. The hoist begins and we're rising slowly toward the helicopter — nice feeling! I know it's very hard for the pilot: he has to watch like a hawk that he doesn't get too close to the raft or onto the rocks while we're getting pulled up.

Photo courtesy of Norm Penny.

At last we're in the chopper. The fisherman I've brought up is straight away looked after in the back of the aircraft. As for me: I've swallowed a lot of water. I've thrown up, and don't feel in very good shape.

The crew looks at me. They look again at the whole situation. The hoist I'd done was very hard, and the rest will be the same. But I must go down again. I have to try to get some of the others. After that, we'll just have to pull away or we'll be in danger ourselves. These rocky coasts are really treacherous. The weather often wild — like now.

I'm lying on the floor of the chopper. I can feel how time's passing. Somehow I have to get up; I must get on my feet and do this thing. Below me are fishermen. They're about to drown or hit the rocks, and if they do, they'll all die. I struggle upright and get ready to go. I think

Norm Penny and Derek Rogers stand beside a Canadian Coast Guard rescue helicopter.

maybe I'm okay. The crew lowers me. I get close to the raft and that's when things get a bit hairy. I think the pilot is worried. He can't see the rocks because of the blackness of the night. He lunges the chopper forward but there's not enough slack on the cable and it picks me up out of the water. I'm bounced on top of the raft. I hit the roof, then the other side of it. Next minute I'm airborne again and pulled to the other side of the raft. Then I hit the water hard. All I can do is roll up and put my head to my knees. Now, in a kind of backward motion, I'm yanked in the opposite direction. It feels like I'm tied to a car and being dragged down the road — a horrible kind of tumbling action.

‖‖‖‖‖‖‖‖‖‖‖‖

From the raft, the sailors are watching.

149

"Oh my God, I seen the rescue guy, and he's dead." One of them stares into the menacing swells of the ocean to see Norm being violently pulled. "That guy, he's being yanked through the water … he's got pulled through the water and he's killed."

The men stare at each other. They are all thinking the same — that the rescue team had killed one of their own. Now they themselves are really on their own.

The crew in the chopper can't see Norm. All they see is the strange angle to the cable. They look at each other in dismay. There's nothing they can do but cut it. If they don't, they'll keep dragging him about and risk breaking his neck. Then what will happen to him? They have no communication with him; they can't even see him.

In the water, Norm surfaces. When the bubbles clear, he sees that the cable has been cut and he's separated from the aircraft. He's alone in a black and ugly sea with no dive mask and no swimming fins. He believes the cut cable is still attached to him — all hundred feet of it — and it's pulling him down. All the time he's getting closer to the jagged shore. He figures he's only about 400 metres from it.

From the aircraft, Derek sees there is a malfunction and can only watch helplessly as the cable attached to Norm, together with 100 feet of stowed backup cable, drops as though in slow motion, all the way to the bottom of the ocean.

Norm's dry suit is torn. His scuba fins are blown off, the soles of his shoes half torn off, and his mask shattered. The weight of the now-bent hook pulls him underwater. Frantically he fights to get it off him so he can come up for air. He's got his head above water. He can see the yellow light of the chopper; can see its strobe lights. But its crew can't see him. They've lost him. They don't know where he is. For both Norm, and for the crew in the helicopter, these are very bad moments. Norm believes he's drowning — but he can't drown! He has to survive, he must survive … there's his little girl … a little girl needs her dad …

Fear and dismay mark the faces of the crew in the chopper; they can't believe what has just happened, the situation they are now facing.

"Okay, guys, just calm down," Derek says. "Here's a new plan. We'll go from a raft hoist to a mountain rescue. This is now officially a mountain rescue."

Norm, in the water, doesn't know that both cables are gone. He believes he's still attached to one of them. He bends his head into the water to try to remove the hook that ties him to it.

"But where's the raft?" he frets. "I can't see it ... the swell's too big ... the flashlight, where's the flashlight? I have to get out of here! I have to find the chopper."

Up in the helicopter, Derek's anxiety for Norm increases with each passing moment. He stares into the roiling ocean from the craft's open doorway.

"There he is!" he yells suddenly. "I can see Norm's head." But Norm is face down in the water. He's not moving. Derek's fear for his partner surges. Without regard to his own injuries and his own ripped survival suit, he jumps up. Risking his own life, he puts on his face mask and fins and gets himself ready for a front-door entry to jump down to him.

"I'm going to get my partner."

"But your suit is ripped ... there's no hoist left to get you out ..."

"I don't care! I have to get to him, turn him over!"

Suddenly Norm's head pops up above the water, and there is a light. It has to be Norm's light signal; it must be his signal. Norm must be okay! Relief floods over Derek like a huge surging tide.

"Don't lose sight of him!" he says swiftly to the crew. "Make sure you stay over him!"

The pilot struggles to keep his craft hovering in the area where Norm's head has been spotted, but it's perilously close to the cliffs. The feat he's been asked to do is almost impossible: Winds are blowing at 55 knots; the rain is very hard-hitting. He must keep the chopper above the ocean's 30-foot swells and away from the rocks — all this in the absolute blackness of night.

"Get the belay kit from the shelf," Derek yells. "Thank God we decided not to strip the craft." Someone grabs the kit and ties it securely to the helicopter. Derek grins suddenly. This is something they are doing that's not found in any safety and security manual.

Norm has been face down in the water, struggling to unhook himself from the cable. He looks up to see where the chopper is. It looks dark and far away from him. Frantically he tries to communicate with it using light signals. He keeps hitting it with his flashlight, and as he does, he remembers Derek tying it onto him before he'd jumped.

Thanks, Derek! he says silently.

Up in the aircraft, Derek is watching like a hawk. "Keep your eyes on him," he orders his crew once more. "Whatever you do, don't lose him. Don't lose him! We've got no hooks left but I'm going to rig up a rope."

The crew lowers a collar down for Norm to grab and hook onto himself. It drops, but the winds blow it right back to the rear of the helicopter. There is no hoist left so the only choice now is to send the basket down. Attached to a rope, the basket drops about 20 feet from Norm. But he can't swim to it — he's lost his fins.

"Okay, we'll try again," says Derek, not trying to hide his frustration. On the second attempt the basket lands 10 feet away from Norm. Still he can't swim to it. On the third try the basket hits him on the head. He crawls into it and yells, "Pick me up, get me out of here!" At first he believes he's being hoisted. He's not. What has come down to him is a rope.

Okay, I'm not getting hoisted. Something must be wrong with the hoist.

But he's in the basket. He can hear the chopper. It's getting close; it's landing in a small tight spot on the road above the cliffs in a gusting wind. Norm is long-lined to the nearest shore, the crew using everything and anything they can. He's landed smoothly on a small, narrow road with traffic lined up on each side.

"The split second I'm on the ground I get myself out of the basket," Norm says. "For some reason I notice the view of the town of Bonavista. I see all the locals and how they've come out for this drama. The crew has put my sorry butt down in a very small spot. They've had to do it in crazy weather. I worry for them. This is not any kind of a place for a chopper to land. I run to clear my equipment from the road to make it easier for them. Then I run with my gear and the basket on my back, straight toward someone's car lights — I'm sure he doesn't know what's coming at him! I feel safe now. It's the boys in the helicopter who are in danger because of where they have to come down."

The chopper lands. Before the wheels touch down and the aircraft can settle, Derek is out running and saying, "Are you all right, man?"

The two SAR Techs smile at each other. "We know it's been a ride," Norm says. "And we know it's not over yet."

Norm takes off his carabiner and puts it down at the rescue door. That's when he sees Derek's invention.

"What's this?" Norm stares.

"That's how we got you back."

Norm feels his heart dropping in amazement. The rope lying coiled over the floor of the helicopter looks like a giant spider web. It has been his lifeline out of the ocean.

"It's a rope — it's how we rescued you."

"A rope — I thought it was a hoist!"

Norm forgets that the soles of his boots have been torn away, that he is near barefoot and almost bleeding, that he's bruised and sick with all the water he's swallowed. As though nothing has happened, he joins the crew in making plans about what they will do now. How they will get the men out of the life raft and up the cliffs.

FASCINATING FACT
Rescue Lingo: A Helicopter Long-line Rescue

A long-line rescue is used when there are no other means of removing an injured person from an inaccessible place; when a helicopter cannot be shut down while the patient is loaded on board. Both doors are removed or snapped back; a special nylon rope — a belly band — is placed through the open doors around the floor of the helicopter. This belly band has a releasable latch located on the floor at the spotter's feet, and it is also connected to the helicopter's pilot-controlled releasable hook by a nylon strap called the Y lanyard. This attaches at two points to the helicopter. In the event of an emergency, the pilot tells the spotter to release the belly band, and the total weight of the rescue long-line is then transferred to the helicopter's hook. The pilot can then release the hook — electronically or manually — at an appropriate moment and those attached to the long-line are placed on the ground before the line is released. It is arranged this way because of the risks: equipment being snagged in rocks or trees; loss of power; or the need for the pilot to make an emergency crash landing.

Imagine a 200-foot rope with a stretcher at the end of it, the patient secured inside. On each side hangs a rescuer, feet dangling but hands relatively free, rigged up so that he can compress the chest, then switch over to squeeze the bag and ventilate the lifeless patient.

Imagine trapeze artists performing delicate manoeuvres while suspended at the end of a rope, with no safety net. If they were to fall, they would die.

FASCINATING FACT
What Is a Carabiner?

A carabiner is an oblong metal ring with a spring clip that can be opened or closed. It is used to attach ropes to anchors or to make quick connections with ropes and tapes. It was originally a device used in rock climbing but is now used in many different types of rescues. The word is short for *Karabinerhaken*, meaning "hook for a carbine" in German.

The rescued sailor who has been cared for at the rear of the craft is about to be transferred to the local hospital. News comes from the RCMP that the remaining sailors have washed up on shore. At this very moment they're lying huddled on rocks at the base of the cliffs.

Derek and Norm look at each other.

"We have to get these guys," each says to the other. "We've just *got* to get them. So, okay, now we're into ground rescue mode."

It is decided that the two SAR Techs will join other rescuers who have arrived at the cliff top. Somehow they will get themselves down to the sailors and bring them up. But the spot where they've washed up is some distance down the shoreline. The two SAR Techs have to get there fast.

"Prepare the mountain and medical kits," Derek says to Norm. He races outside to try to track down a local person with a truck.

"Just like something out of the movies," Norm says, and laughs.

"We need your truck," Derek yells at the driver. "We need a ride to get down the road a bit to the cliffs …"

"Jump on," the driver says. Norm and Derek jump. They get a tailgate ride to the area of the cliffs close to the spot where the sailors have washed up. Many people have already gathered at this spot, all wanting to know if they can help.

"We're hoping that by the time we get there these people will have some good news," Norm says. "We're hoping other rescuers will have got all the men up. The people's eyes slam on us as we're running down the road in our red fluorescent suits and all our ropes. My heart lifts because now we're right back in business. We can see Search and Rescue people already there. The RCMP and local firefighters are there. Right now they're bringing one sailor up from the shore. Derek and I begin preparing a rescue system to go get another one."

One sailor lies on rocks 80 feet below, down a cliff face. It's all rock and shale. It's steep. It's wet and slippery. When it's touched it just crumbles! — Now what to do?

Undaunted, the two SAR Techs look about for anchor points — for something to tie the ropes to: There's nothing. They run into the crowds. They look about wildly, then head toward a group of men standing beside their four wheelers (quads).

"We need help!" Derek is simultaneously commanding and begging. "Can we use your quads?" Almost without pausing, the two SAR Techs tie ropes through the quad wheels. Next they make a harness. "Jump on your quads to give them extra weight," he orders. "I'll operate the system we've rigged up," he says to Norm. "I've got the most experience. You'll be lowered down to the sailor."

Everything gets checked. Derek gives him the thumbs-up, and Norm goes over the cliff. He looks over his shoulder to check his route. A flare is dropped and he gets a good look at the conditions he's getting into, but it's a bit hard to see anything in the blackness of the night. One flare does manage to penetrate the darkness, and it's then he sees what's below him: a roiling sea smashing onto the rocks, white spray spinning high into the air. It seems like a giant washing machine and he wished he hadn't looked.

With near-bare and bruised feet, Norm climbs down a dangerously unstable cliff face. As he goes over, he talks to Derek who hears him mutter, "Okay, I'm going down, down ... I've reached the bottom ... stop!"

He has to somehow get down to the sailor he can now see at the bottom. He has to do it without knocking loose rocks on him. Already he can see that the poor fellow is in no condition to climb up without help — as if anyone could! Norm carefully picks his way over the cliff, hands and fingers sore and bleeding, feet with little protection. Time is suspended. Eventually he reaches the rocky platform where the sailor lies. A glance tells him the man is almost dead with cold and exhaustion. He sees other sailors clinging to the rock with their fingernails and toes.

"The rain's coming down like a river. If I slip I'm going to knock these guys another 20 feet down the cliff ... at last I'm at the bottom. I'm here with one of the fishermen. 'Hey, you're going to live!' I tell him. At first he just grabbed me. I said, 'Don't do that, it's dangerous.' I put a diaper-like harness with three rings about him. The poor man: he'd fought so hard for his life that when he knows he's rescued, he just lets go. He puts everything in my hands.

"Derek is set to begin the raise to the top. The rope is being jerked and then shortened. But communication is poor. Radios are not working in this particular spot. I'm shouting, but can't make my voice heard above waves crashing on the rocks and the thrashing rain. So we go old school — we use bells and whistles. It's something useful I learned from Fleet Diving Unit (FDU) training. Now we're being stretched, we're pulled up to the top."

Getting up the cliff is slow and difficult. It is a treacherous cliff face, and the sailor can't help himself. Norm too is extremely fatigued. At last he reaches the top and hands the sailor over to Emergency Medical Services personnel. He hears that another sailor has managed to get himself up by himself — great!

There is a shout, *I can see someone else!* Another man is spotted in a different area of the cliffs, a place not as steep, and easier to reach. The rope-lowering system is not needed. This time Derek climbs down the cliffs. He pulls the sailor up, hand over hand.

"One of us didn't make it ..." the sailor begins, but his words are cut off by a shout that another man has been spotted in the light shining from Tusker's flares that have punched through the clouds. What they are seeing is a reflection from his watch. Without this flare, the fortunate man would never have been found in the blackness of both the evening and his clothes. He huddles on rocks 80 feet below as pounding surf flies up and over his rocky ledge. Derek sets up an anchor and rope system, and the fourth sailor is pulled up the cliffs.

The dead man remains on rocks at the base of the cliffs, but the rescue effort has to be called off. The weather is poor and rapidly deteriorating. Norm and Derek secure the unfortunate man's body at the bottom of the rocks so it won't wash away, and the two finally climb back to the top of the cliffs.

The rescue team is about to enter the RCMP station when news comes of a light flashing some distance away. A search is made — it must belong to one other sailor still down there. The rescue team returns to the cliffs and Norm goes down once more with the rescue basket. At the cliff bottom lies a big man with a desperate will to survive. Norm struggles with him up the cliffs.

"There's just one more sailor," Norm says. He waits with the team; cold, sore, and exhausted. Forty-five minutes pass before they give up and head for a hotel.

"I got to a hotel and called my wife," Norm says "I called a buddy of mine — I just had to talk to someone. Next, a hot shower and a warm bed — it felt so good. But sleep was impossible. All night I lay staring at the ceiling."

Norm and Derek have endured an ordeal that has left them cold, hypothermic, and pretty roughed up. They are bruised and bleeding, and both have swallowed a lot of water. Because of their harrowing experience, they are grounded from flying for a week.

The rescued sailors have something of their own to say.

"We were terrified, and most of us near dead in our raft," one said. "We watched a Search and Rescue guy try to get to us and bring us up. We watched him get dashed against our raft. We saw him get yanked about in the air. Next thing he's disappeared under the big swells. We believe he's dead. We think they killed one of their own."

"Then when I washed ashore," Norm says, "I'm the first man they see coming down the cliffs. One of the fishermen whispers, 'I seen a ghost!'"

ıııııııııııııııııı

During this search and rescue operation, two SAR Technicians went out to rescue six stranded fishermen, but the team had to rescue one of their own. Both technicians were beaten and bruised. They came close to losing their own lives. Almost barefoot, their suits ripped, they went back to rescue another and another in a tropical storm of hurricane winds and howling rain.

"We never gave up. We gave more than the call of duty," Norm says. "I have pride in that. When we went out to get these guys, we went above and beyond. I also want to say that Derek Rogers is the reason why I'm here today — he saved my life."

Norm Penny has been a SAR Tech for five years and in the Army for eight.

He uses words like *patriotism* and *pride* in serving his country.

"There is honour in being in the Army," he says. "This work gives me the opportunity to believe in and to stand for something. It's a good feeling. I'm proud to be a soldier, and I'm good at it."

"Eighty to ninety percent of Search and Rescue Technicians go into the Army first," he says. "It gives you structure and good physical training. It suited me. I was raised by

FASCINATING FACT
Search and Rescue Technicians: Who Are They?

SAR Techs are specialists in rescue, survival, and emergency medical aid. They are trained to participate in searches for downed planes and to parachute in to crash sites to aid the survivors.

Training includes day and night jumps from altitudes as low as about 350 metres, and takes place at Namao, although 435 SAR Squadron moved to Winnipeg in 1994. Medical training is carried out at University Hospital emergency ward where crash victims are brought.

Equipment includes: all first-aid equipment; gasoline-fired stoves; tents; sleeping bags; radios; emergency rations — and climbing gear in the event they have to walk out in mountainous terrain.

In Canada, there are not many paid careers exclusively in Search and Rescue (SAR). Since "heavy duty" Search and Rescue requires specialized training and equipment, most primary SAR services are housed in larger organizations such as the Canadian Forces (Air Force.), the Canadian Coast Guard, and police and fire departments.

The Canadian Forces elite Search and Rescue Technicians (SAR Techs) are highly trained specialists who respond as aviators, mariners, and others within the military's SAR system. They are comfortable operating in any environment. In addition to being qualified in advanced trauma life support, they are also skilled at diving, parachuting, mountain climbing, and rappelling. To become a SAR Tech in the Canadian Forces, four years of service in another military trade are normally required.

The Canadian Forces also has skilled pilots, navigators, and other air crew that are specially trained in the SAR role, operating helicopters and fixed-wing aircraft across Canada.

my grandmother with good old-fashioned manners and do-what-you're-told discipline. By the time I was 13, I was a cadet. I enjoyed sports and physical challenges, with the adrenaline pumping. In a few years I was into the Army because I always wanted to do military stuff — there's a gung-ho thing you feel, and you represent your country.

"We do everything; mountain climbing for rescues, medical help, boating, parachuting, scuba diving, helicopter hoisting … we do our best to save lives."

"I like being a service person because it all comes down to honour. Like, every day when I put on my uniform, a Canadian flag on my left shoulder, I know that I stand for something. I know I'm going to help, to be at the beck and call of others, and serve them."

Sergeant Derek Rogers and Master Corporal Norm Penny received the Star of Courage for risking their lives to save the drowning fishermen during the storm. "We train for what we do, then go out and do it," Rogers said.

"I'm the luckiest guy in the Canadian Forces," Penny said. "I have the chance to return loved ones to their families … it shows Canadians they have a resource when they need help in this vast country with its challenging landscapes and changing climates. It allows us as SAR Techs to represent all SAR personnel and all who wear the Forces uniform to show the flag, and let all Canadian citizens know that we are there for them. Rescue!"

Derek Rogers and Norm Penny were awarded the Star of Courage. This honour was instituted in 1972, a middle-level award for Canadian Bravery Decorations. It is given only for acts of conspicuous courage in circumstances of great peril.

Sergeant Rogers has recently been relocated to Afghanistan, the first SAR Tech to operate in a combat environment.

Photo courtesy of Norm Penny.

Derek Rogers and Norm Penny receive the Star of Courage from the governor general of Canada.

11 The World's Last Great Wilderness

It happened deep in the heart of winter when snow lay in huge white drifts; when clouds seemed to drop from the sky and hang like white party streamers on the spruce branches. Four young men in their teens and early twenties made plans for a weekend party. They would ride off on their snowmobiles to a lonely cottage owned by the father of one of them. A temperature of minus 58 degrees Celsius was of no concern. When warned of a blizzard that would hit within 24 hours, they shrugged.

The shack, 20 kilometres from the town of Wabush, stood half-hidden in a heavily wooded, isolated spot. The only path to it was a snowmobile trail that wound through hills and valleys of pure clean snow; through drifts that piled high among the trees. The perfect spot for a winter weekend party, the young people thought. A place to eat and drink, to joke about, have some laughs, to play good music and kid around — all away from adult eyes.

They packed plenty of food and beer then roared off on their snowmobiles into the bitter cold.

Later the same day, three other young men set off to join the party. Not owning snowmobiles, they hired a taxi to drive them over the ten kilometres of rough gravel road from town. When the road ended and the ground became impassable by car, they began a long, cold walk for the last ten kilometres. The conditions meant little to them since they were used to Labrador's weather. They had no fear of getting disoriented and lost in the vast white forest.

The lonely cottage crouched among the trees, far from a road, far from any other dwelling, and far from any hint that any other life in the world existed. The cottage was furnished with two horsehair armchairs and a worn carpet flung over crooked floorboards. A portable AM radio and a stereo system sat on a table, and old books and magazines lay scattered on rough shelves near the wood-burning stove. Two iron bedsteads and bunks, with rugs, pillows, and thick, downy throws piled on them, filled the two small bedrooms. Tattered cotton drapes hung at the windows.

Winds howled about the small building and blew snow hard up against the windows. Views of the outside world — lake, trees, the snowmobile trail — were invisible.

Happy to be away from adults, the four whistled and kidded each other. Some unloaded food and beer while others found board games and playing cards. The chill of the air indoors was not much different from the outside world, but they told themselves it wouldn't take long to get the place heated. In the meantime, there was much stamping of feet and jumping about to try to get warm.

Time passed. The friends did not arrive. The partiers kept going to the door and peering out. The storm swirled even more fiercely and the four young men became increasingly restive and bored. They also began to feel a little uneasy inside the rough little cabin where they had no glimpse of the outside world.

Anxious about their buddies, they ventured out several times, fired up their snowmobiles and slowly crossed the lonely trails in search of them.

The night passed, and a long and boring day. By evening the four were discouraged by the increasing winds and falling temperatures, and also by the fact that their friends had not shown up. All they could think was that their friends had been put off by the weather. They decided to pack up and get back to town. Disappointed, they travelled the twisting trails through the woods, back to the road, and to the town.

At home they telephoned the friends who were supposed to have joined them, to boast about what a good time they'd had. To their astonishment, they heard the friends had indeed set out to join them at the cottage. Nobody had seen or heard from them since. A deafening silence followed this news, until someone said, "If they're lost out there, heaven help them."

These and other words were muttered as a series of frantic phone calls bounced along the telephone wires to every person and place where the missing men could possibly be. The police were notified, and within a short time, the town's volunteer search team was called out.

||||||||||||||||||||

That evening, Craig Porter drove down his quiet residential street in Wabush as an Arctic wind whipped around corners of the rows of small bungalows and duplexes that seemed to huddle together against its cruel bite. Craig pulled into his driveway. Before entering his home he plugged the vehicle's block heater into an electrical outlet to keep its engine warm. His wife, Lori, was in the kitchen. He sniffed at the smells that drifted down the hallway to greet him. He smiled at the sight of seven-year-old Emily Rose seated at the dining table, homework spread out on it.

Craig loved opening the door to be greeted by the warmth and comfort of a scene like this. It was the reason he liked his day job as a mechanic in the local iron ore mines — because it left evenings free to spend time at home with his family.

"Not a time to be outdoors," he said to Lori. "I wouldn't put my dog out in it."

Scarcely had he sat down in the coziness of his living room to watch television with the family when the phone rang. Craig glanced at his wife and his daughter, shrugged, and picked it up. The message sent chills down his spine.

"Search and rescue — gotta go," he said. "Three young fellows lost in the woods way out near Mills Lake. They were to be at a cottage nearby but never made it. We'll find them." This last was stated with confidence.

Craig's outdoor gear and his search and rescue bag hung in a closet by the front door. He snatched them up, was out the door, in his truck, and gone in a few moments.

He and other SAR volunteers contacted by the police headed for the police precinct on the outskirts of Labrador City. As he raced his truck along the deserted roads toward the outskirts of the town, Craig's mind was filled with dread.

Thirty-nine SAR members roared into the parking lot and piled into the police station. A sense of foreboding hung in the air. Darkness was falling, and three young men had been missing since early the day before. Under the direction of

> ## FASCINATING FACT
> ### Royal Newfoundland Constabulary
>
> "Police" in this instance refers to the Royal Newfoundland Constabulary. It polices the province of Newfoundland and Labrador. Since the 1860s it has been the force of choice for the city of St. John's, but has since broadened its jurisdiction to include most of the Avalon Peninsula and the city of Corner Brook. Since 1984 it has assumed policing duties in Labrador City, Wabush, and Churchill.

Craig Giles, an officer of the Royal Newfoundland Constabulary, the volunteers were grouped into four teams of four searchers each, and a police officer was assigned to each team. All four groups were provided with portable police telephones. Craig Porter's team included his hunting partner Eugene Joy, and a young rookie cop about to venture out on his first trip on a snowmobile in Labrador. It was a strange scene: the massing of machines and their helmeted, heavily cloaked drivers in the stillness of this bitter evening. Machines were cranked up and, with a roar, two of the teams headed overland along an old surveyors' trail to check out the cottage the missing men had tried to reach. The other two teams visited every cottage near the road. It meant stopping at all dwellings. Regardless of signs of use or disuse, they dismounted, trudged through heavy snow, knocked, and then shouted at each silent door. Before leaving imprints of their own presence, each searched the ground for any sign that the young people had stopped there.

As the night got blacker, the temperature — which had registered minus 58 when they'd first left town — had dropped to minus 87 with the wind chill factored in. It was a slow and miserable job. Physical exhaustion added to the anxiety they all felt.

An exhaustive search spanning two hours failed to turn up any evidence of the men. No prints or smudges disturbed virgin snow piled about the trees and in black hollows. No evidence — such as dropped beer bottles or food wrappers — was found.

Two teams met at a fork in the trail. What now? What had any of them found? With cold-stiffened fingers, one of the searchers pulled out his radio to tell the command post they hadn't found anything and to ask what they should do next. They milled about trying to generate some body heat, all the while continuing to scan the ground for signs of life that might have passed that way. The job was made very difficult because of falling and drifting snow.

Suddenly a shout shot through the trees and a voice yelled, "Hey, take a look at this!"

The forest fell silent for a fraction of a second. A crunching of boots in the snow then filled it, a rush of bodies to the spot where a searcher bent over, examining half-buried footprints.

Hope flared in the hearts of the rescuers. Re-energized, they immediately took to their snowmobiles. Back again to the numbing task of following an almost nonexistent trail deeper and deeper into the nearly impenetrable wilds of Labrador.

Many pairs of eyes anxiously scanned the deadened white world as the searchers moved carefully through it. Each searcher frantically looked for evidence that life had existed here — even for one brief moment — before passing on. Shouts rang intermittently in the eerie silence of the trees when someone thought they had discovered evidence of a spot where the three might have flopped — perhaps to summon up reserves of energy to recoup flagging spirits.

"As we got deeper and deeper into the night in a wind that bit into us, and a cold that stung, then numbed even the hardiest among us, we wondered in our hearts if the next bend in the trail would bring us face to face with a group of bodies all slumped together," Craig Porter said afterward. Like so many rescuers, he hoped to find bodies — but only those that were still breathing.

Two hours, and 17 kilometres from the road, one team came upon another fork in the trail. Four searchers were left at the junction of these two trails to build a fire, while two other searchers and a police officer set off, each in a different direction, to keep looking. Severe cold had begun to exact a toll on all.

Craig, Eugene, and the rookie officer proceeded carefully along the surveyors' line trail until they came to Molar Lake, about half a kilometre away. There was no sign of footprints or any clues that told them others had been there before. Hearts grew heavy and hope plummeted. Upon reaching the lake, searchers began a series of zigzag patterns across its frozen surface, trying to cut across any existing trail the lost men might have left behind.

"We were out some several hundred yards on the lake and came across deep holes in the surface snow that covered the ice," said Craig. "We stopped to take a look to try to figure out what it meant. Amazing really that we found these marks at all — mostly they were buried by blowing snow."

They were indeed footprints, and joy would have gladdened the hearts of the men had it not been for a terrible twist: slush was discovered!

"Slush: it's a deep layer of water between the ice and the covering snow," explained Craig. "These conditions made walking much harder, with the added danger of searchers suffering frozen feet in the extreme temperatures."

The group pushed on, slush adding a renewed sense of urgency. They understood that the three lost men must be in serious trouble. Unless of course they'd found some kind of shelter in the 24 hours since they'd been dropped off by their taxi driver. The trail now wavered from side to side. Anyone disoriented in this weird white world would not know that the actual trail they'd intended to follow was some 12 kilometres behind them.

"As we neared the far end of the lake, our spirits sank again," Craig said. "We knew the three had not found shelter; that they were about to enter the woods, and then the endless trails beyond. We were thinking the worst when we came around a small point that jutted out into the lake. We swung around it, adrenaline pumping and still thinking the worst: a collective nightmarish vision of bodies slumped in the snow. What we saw was a flicker of light! We couldn't believe it. Some shouted their excitement and we all rushed toward it. Our hopes soared high. We hoped … prayed …

"And then the unbelievable happened; we saw three men huddling about a small stove. Their clothes were flung on its pipe to dry. We shouted and yelled all at the same time — you should have heard. Oh, man, it was great! These were our neighbours; our buddies, friends and family. We'd found them alive."

"We're members of the Labrador West Ground Search and Rescue team," one of the searchers said at last. He tried to stretch a smile across his frozen face. "We've been looking all over for you."

"Thank God! Are we ever glad to see you! Thank you, thank you, thank you!" Smiles of relief etched across the visible part of their frozen faces.

Craig radioed to tell the remaining team members that the men had been found. Not long afterward, the other teams roared up to the forsaken spot in the woods.

The three lost men were checked for injuries. Rescuers took the opportunity to warm themselves up by the stove — to refuel before beginning the long trek back to the road.

"We thought we'd missed the trail," said one of the wayward cottagers. "But we kept going in the hopes that our buddies were on their way to get us. Yeah, we were exhausted. And, oh man, we thought we were near dead. At the end — you know? But we kept pressing on. Had to stop often to rest — we had to."

"We left our beer buried in the snow — too exhausted to carry it any further," said another, with a wry grin on his face. "When we came to the lake, we kept on going because we thought we were almost there. Then we began to think *this is it, we're done for.* We just didn't have it in us to go any further. That's when we came upon a trapper's cabin, and how we got through the night."

With no provisions, the men were preparing to walk out the next morning. But without the search party, in the deteriorating weather, their trek out into an endless, frozen world was a tragedy waiting to happen.

Why, Craig Porter was asked later, does he put himself at additional risk? Isn't life here in this harsh climate tough enough without making it even more dangerous?

"Well, let me tell you," he said. "When I'm a young fellow and just turned 21, I go fishing with a friend called Joe Snow. We stay in a cabin near a small lake to see what we could get — and you know — have a good time. I'm in the kayak on the lake, going after brook trout. I haul up a stringer full of fish — about 14 of them. The stringer gets untied from the kayak and the fish swim away. I'm reaching out for the stringer, and I tip over the kayak.

"Joe's standing in the doorway of the cabin, watching me. He drops his coffee, runs for the aluminum boat on the shore, and rows it the 100 feet or so to get to me — he takes five minutes — or less. Already I'm so numbed with cold that I can't haul myself into the boat, and he can't pull me in without capsizing. So he ties a rope around one of my wrists and tows me to shore. Hypothermia? Oh, yeah. The lakes are always freezing. I would have been a dead man within minutes if he hadn't been there. Joe cranks up a good fire, puts me in a down-filled sleeping bag, and I'm okay. But I never forgot it — forgot how I was rescued. I knew what my fate would've been had Joe not been there.

"I wanted to do the same for others," he added. "When you put yourself out, even endanger yourself to rescue someone, it's almost like you've given life. It makes you feel you're doing some worthwhile thing."

He paused, grinned, and then added, "It's easy to get into trouble here. Way back in 1984, three years after my accident, I saw an advertisement in the local paper inviting people to join with the police in an auxiliary capacity for search and rescue. I remembered the time when I got rescued from the lake and I thought *this is how I can get trained to rescue other people who get in trouble*. So I volunteered and got accepted into a search and rescue training program. Now I can go searching for missing people anywhere, in any weather — and let me tell you, the climate here is very unforgiving for a good part of each year."

Craig undertook more courses so that, after a successful search, he would know how to resuscitate and revive the people he rescued. His intensive training also qualified him to assist the local police on search and rescue calls.

For 16 years, he has made himself available, put himself permanently on call for search and rescue. It's meant that he must be prepared to stop whatever he's doing, regardless of whether it's his work in the mines, his personal recreation, or his family life. He must drop everything, gear up, and go to remote places to search for missing people or to recover those believed to be dead. He understood he would often have to travel in the most difficult winter weather, to suffer extreme cold, possible frostbite and hypothermia, physical injury, and exhaustion.

"To do rescue work has become my life's passion; there's no feeling quite like it in the world," he said. "Nothing makes my day like having a search coming to a successful conclusion, the missing person hugging their family when we get back to the command post."

He explained that young people in Labrador are familiar with the perils of their environment. They do not disregard them, but they refuse to let them stop doing the things

FASCINATING FACT
More About Labrador

Labrador is a region of Atlantic Canada and together with the island of Newfoundland forms the province of Newfoundland and Labrador, known by the Norse as Markland. The population in 2006 was 26,364 and included 30 percent Aboriginal Peoples: Inuit, Innu, and Métis. Its size is 294,330 square kilometres. The name Markland dates back almost as far as Newfoundland, so named after João Fernandes Lavrador and Péro de Barcelos sighted it in 1498.

Labrador, the place for which Craig expresses such passion, is the northern territory of the province of Newfoundland. Labrador City and Wabush lie on the extreme western border, near Quebec. The bulk of this land is a vast wilderness. One can see forever. In the north, there is tundra, and in the south, vast timber stands.

One of the last great wilderness areas of the Earth it, it boasts towering mountain ranges, massive rock faces, lakes, and teeming rivers. Wildlife runs free: moose, caribou, giant Arctic hares, lynx, polar bears, porcupines, and wolves. Its remote nature protects it from most forms of encroachment by modern society. The place is unforgiving with long, frigid winters, high snowfall, harsh terrain, and extreme isolation.

When Craig Porter speaks of sports, and the physical challenges that go with them, he refers to the excellent alpine and cross-country skiing, and particularly snowmobiling. The season for this activity is very long. Wilderness trails are breathtaking and extensive. Few who have visited would dispute that this is one of the planet's unspoiled places.

Craig is at home in this harsh natural world, and enjoys its challenges. An added dimension to his life that is distinct from his home, his work, and all his outdoor recreational pursuits, is the volunteer search and rescue work he does for the Royal Newfoundland Constabulary. In 2008 he received the McGregor Volunteer of the Year Award from the town of Wabush for exemplifying the spirit of volunteerism through his dedication and commitment.

they love to do. They unconsciously absorb into their lives the hazards of extreme weather, temperature, and isolation. But no matter how careful, no matter what precautions they take, they know that accidents can easily happen and that unforeseen circumstances occur.

They know, and still they play. What else can they do? The landscape and the climate will always be there. Young people will not remain indoors on a wintry night when the temperature falls to levels incompatible with life if it means giving up a party, a hunting trip, or a snowmobile adventure in the great white outdoors. Many love the challenge, the beating of the odds, the physical thrill.

"For myself, I love this place," Craig says of Wabush in particular and of Labrador in general. "My parents brought me here when I was six years old — and my three sisters and brother, of course. I've been here for 36 years, and I never want to leave. "Here is everything a person could ever want in life. I have a good steady job as an industrial mechanic in the nearby iron ore mines. I go fishing for lake and brook trout, sometimes for northern pike and *ouaniniche* — that's a landlocked species of salmon. I hunt for rabbit, grouse, bear, and caribou — but never for sport, only to feed the family. We all go snowmobiling and get involved in all the sports here. It's a great life in the huge outdoors — lots of physical challenges.

"What else could a person want? I don't think there is any place else like it in the world."

Photo courtesy of Norm Penny.

A Search and Rescue Technician is hoisted back up into a hovering helicopter.

Resources

Selected Books

Matthews, Carolyn. *Heroic Rescues at Sea: True Stories of the Canadian Coast Guard*. Halifax, Nova Scotia: Nimbus Publishing, 2002.

Matthews, Carolyn. *To the Rescue: True Stories of Tragedy and Survival*. Toronto: Dundurn Press, 2005.

Melady, John. *Heartbreak and Heroism: Canadian Search and Rescue Stories*. Toronto: Dundurn Press, 1997.

Melady, John. *Star of Courage: Recognizing the Heroes Among Us*. Toronto: Dundurn Press, 2001.

Selected Websites

Canada Task Force One (Vancouver Urban Search and Rescue): *www.can_tf1.org*

Canada's Air Force, Search and Rescue: *www.airforce.forces.gc.ca/site/athomedocs/athome_2_e. asp*

Canadian Coast Guard: *www.ccg-gcc.gc.ca*

Canadian Forces School of Search and Rescue (CFSSAR): *www.airforce.forces.gc.ca/19wing/squadron/cfssr_e.asp*

Civil Air Search and Rescue Association (CASARA): *www.casara.ca*

Joint Rescue Coordination Centre (JRCC): *www.airforce.*forces*.gc.ca8wing/squadron/jrcc_e.asp*

Labrador West Ground Search and Rescue Team: *www.crrstv.net/jcporter*

Newfoundland and Labrador Search and Rescue Association (NLSARA): *www.nlsara.org*

National Search and Rescue Secretariat: *www.nss.gc.ca*

North Shore Rescue (NSR), Mountain Search and Rescue Team: *www.northshorerescue.com*

Royal Canadian Mounted Police (RCMP): *www.rcmp-grc.gc.ca*

Sam Steele and the North-West Mounted Police. Library and Archives Canada for kids: *www.collectionscanada.gc.ca/confederation/kids/h2-1645-e.html*

Search and Rescue Dog Association of Alberta (SARDAA): *www.sardaa.ca*

Search and Rescue Society of British Columbia (SARBC): *www.sarbc.org/sarbc/homepage.html*

Search and Rescue Volunteer Association of Canada: *www.sarvac.ca*

Also by Carolyn Matthews

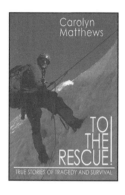

To the Rescue!
True Stories of Tragedy and Survival
978-1-55002-561-3
$24.99

The true stories in this book showcase ordinary people in extraordinary events — a ski accident, a missing child, thrilling sea rescues — that take place from snowbound Labrador to the coast of California.

Of Related Interest:

Heartbreak and Heroism:
Canadian Search and Rescue Stories
by John Melady
978-1-55002-287-2
$29.99

Some of the most dramatic search-and-rescue operations in Canada are recounted here — from the heaving deck of a sinking ship off the Newfoundland coast to high on a British Columbia cliff.

Rescue from Grampa Woo
by Joan Skelton
978-1-896219-45-5
$24.95

This exciting tale of fear and heroism on Lake Superior vividly captures the rescue of two American men from a propellerless cruise ship as it drifted out to sea in hurricane-force winds.

Available at your favourite bookseller

DUNDURN PRESS
www.dundurn.com

Marquis Book Printing Inc.

Québec, Canada
2008